COUPLES OF THE BIBLE

Couples of the Bible

Marcian Strange, O.S.B.

77899

FIDES PUBLISHERS, INC.
NOTRE DAME, INDIANA

Bible quotations are from the new Confraternity of Christian Doctrine translation whenever the books from Genesis to Ruth, Job to Sirach, and Isaiah to Malachiah are cited. When any other book of the Bible is cited, the translations are the author's.

The material in this book first appeared as a series in MARRIAGE magazine, St. Meinrad, Indiana.

Line drawings by Clemens Schmidt.

Library of Congress Catalog Card Number: 63-20805.

for Lew and Della

PREFACE

The Bible was written for our instruction. Does it instruct us as much as it could? The short studies offered in this book aim to open the Bible for readers who want to be instructed by God's word more satisfyingly than they have been in the past. The approach is personal—that is, the studies look at the *persons* who figure in the Bible.

By means of marriage God takes care of man's natural need for complete union with another person and the human race's need for new human life. By marriage God also causes the increase of the supernatural life of grace in baptized persons who involve themselves in this sacrament. The grace of marriage, like all grace, builds on nature *slowly* and *surely.* This is a truth that can come more alive to you as you run through these studies. They will find their mark if they send you searching through the text of the Bible for further reading and reflection.

From the standpoint of literary and doctrinal analysis, very much has been left undone. However, in each study, an effort has been made to find the inspired writer's meaning. Each chapter takes up a different couple and emphasizes one aspect of their lives. A hint is given about the possible relevance of the particular couple to the reader's situation, always with the hope that the reader will go to the Bible itself for more.

TABLE OF CONTENTS

PREFACE

PART ONE

Time of the Patriarchs

Chapter 1

Man and His Rib

ADAM and EVE (Genesis 1-3)

ADAM and Eve—so far away from us they are, and so near. As far away as hundreds of thousands of years, and as near as life's blood in our veins. From these first parents life comes to us as really as from our last parents, the woman who brought us into the world and the man who loved her.

Exactly where and how long ago the earth was first pressed by human feet the Hebrew writer of Genesis did not presume to say. For him, and for us who read his words, the identity of Adam and Eve as individuals often fades and they become a kind of Everyman and Everywoman. Nor did this inspired writer tell precisely how God created them—whether the wonder happened in an instant or after millions of years of animal evolution.

13

This indifference about the time and place and manner of our first parents' origin should not surprise us. The writer of Genesis knew even less about these items than we do, and there was no reason why God should give him the answers. Genesis has a more important message. It teaches us that, no matter how long it took or where it happened, it was God who made the human male and female as the masterpiece of his universe. "God created man in his image. In the image of God he created him. Male and female he created them." Jesus reaffirmed this teaching when he said, "Haven't you read that the Creator from the beginning made them male and female?"

Genesis tells about God's creative activity in a very imaginative way. Like an artist working clay with his hands, God is pictured forming the first man; then, like someone using mouth to mouth—or mouth to nose—respiration, God breathes life into his clay. And there stands Adam.

It would be childish of us to suppose that the writer of Genesis meant that we should take his words as a description of the way God really acts in creating. This writer knew as well as we do that God had no hands to model clay and no lungs or mouth to breathe air. In a simple and imaginative way adapted to the people for whom it was originally written, Genesis tells us that man is a complex of matter (clay) and spirit (God's breath), and that God has made us so.

When it comes to the origin of the human female, Genesis pictures God as a surgeon. God puts his patient Adam to sleep, extracts a rib, and builds it up and out until it is a woman. Here again it would be unfair of us to think that the writer of Genesis meant that the first woman really was a built-up rib that had been lifted from the first man. In his simple and touching way he is telling us that woman is made for man and fits him, and that man is drawn to woman because he feels alone and unfinished without her. She has something important of his within her; she has his heart. She is his rib. And God has made her so.

There they are, naked and unashamed, aware of one another and drawn to one another. Their own nature was saying—and God was speaking in their nature—"Be fruitful and multiply; fill the earth and subdue it." But before their love would be expressed in physical union and before their fruit would ripen into Cain and Abel and Seth, a superhuman enemy of theirs somehow persuaded them to disobey God and lose their friendship with him. This sin, which would have its terrible consequences and its marvelous remedy in the course of time, did not cancel the natural goodness of God's masterpiece. The woman knows that her child is not only from her man but from God. "I have given birth to a man-child with the help of the LORD."

This truth pervades the Catholic Church's teachings on marriage. Sex, and the sexual union of the human male and female, is sacred—like the water used in Baptism and the bread and wine for the Eucharist. The mutual surrender of husband and wife in the union of their bodies has been made by Christ into a sign of something still greater and more filled with wonders, namely his own union with the Church. As Baptism's flowing water is a sign that sin is being washed from the person whom it touches, so the union of husband and wife is a sign that the Church is being united with Christ. The husband's love, which urges him to become one with his wife, is a sign of Christ's love urging him to become one with us. Because of this close connection between human marriage and Christ's union with the Church, Saint Paul wrote: "Husbands, love your wives, just as Christ loved the Church and delivered himself up for her. . . . He who loves his wife loves himself. For no one ever hated his own flesh.

Rather he gives his loving attention to it just as Christ does to the Church."

Married love could never be this sacred sign of Christ's love for us, and Christ's love for us could never be presented as the model of married love, if sex and its use were not good and blessed by God already. For all of us, married and unmarried, this teaching of Genesis is vital to our happiness. Sex, used according to nature's urge and the command of nature's Author—or unused and consecrated to God in imitation of God's Son and in response to his invitation—is a good and wholesome reality of life.

Those of us who teach, in classroom or home, must be alive to this truth. And if warnings must be given against the misuse of sex, let such warnings never cloud over the light of God's truth in the book of Genesis: "God saw that all he had made was very good." When sex is deified in various ways and built up as if it were larger than life, or debased by "free love" into something cheap and therefore incapable of expressing genuine love, or when it is feared as if it were a danger to someone's spiritual life—we need the fresh breeze that blows through the paradise of the first chapters of Genesis.

Chapter 2

Life Is a Gift

NOAH and WIFE   (Genesis 6-9)

WHAT is the modern reader to think when he opens the Bible to the flood story which begins in the 6th chapter of Genesis? He reads of giants who were born of certain "daughters of men" who had become pregnant by mysterious "sons of God," giants who for all their fame became morally corrupt to the point where God regretted ever having made man in the first place and resolved to destroy him.

Then you read that a man named Noah along with his wife and their three sons and their sons' wives were different from other human beings in that they were blameless. This Noah learns from God that he intends to destroy all these other human beings by a world-wide flood and that only Noah and his family will be saved from destruction by means of a huge boat which Noah is to build. Noah builds the boat and gets his family on board along with male and female samples of all the animals and birds of the whole world. The flood comes and the great boat rides high while all other human and animal life is destroyed. The water recedes and Noah and his family get out of the boat to offer a sacrifice to God and to begin again to increase and multiply and fill the empty earth.

17

There may have been a time when Jewish and Christian readers were not in any way bothered by this story but accepted it simply in all its details as factually true—without even wondering how all those cattle and wild animals and birds were ever caught and crammed into one wooden boat. It seems safe to say that most adult believers who read the flood story today wonder a great deal and have many questions in their minds. The part about the giants born of "daughters of men" and "sons of God"—isn't this a piece of Mesopotamian mythology? What is it doing in the Bible except embarrassing people who are wrongly convinced that myth is nothing but the wild imagination of the human race's childhood and that it cannot serve as a vehicle for expressing God's truth? What about the flood itself—its world-wide spread and universal destructive effect? There is no archaeolgical evidence for such a flood. What about the boat? How did all those creatures get into it and how did they all manage to live for 300 days?

No effort will be made here to answer these questions, although reasoned answers can be given. Enough to say here that the writer of Genesis must have been aware of at least some of the difficulties that plague us when we read his text, and that he did not intend his account to be taken as an eye-witness report. His interest in the flood was not so much factual as theological. He is telling us that this catastrophe, whether it was indeed a world-wide flood wiping out almost all human life or a series of disastrous floods in the Tigris-Euphrates valley which semitic tradition had built up imaginatively into a world-wide flood, was God's way of punishing sinful man. By picturing Noah and his family as saved from the otherwise universal destruction, the writer is telling us that God's justice prompts him to make a distinction between blameless and blameworthy human beings—although no explanation is given as to why many innocent lives are destroyed in every such disaster.

Rather than lose our way in this brief look at the flood story, let's center our attention on the main point. God's plan for the human race is based on the family unit, in this case on Noah and his wife. How much of what Genesis says about them was meant to refer to two distinct individuals and how much was meant to refer to good men and women in general—we cannot say. What the inspired writer does teach is that human life, passed on by a man and woman to their children, is God's gift.

Before the flood Genesis has God saying, "My spirit shall not remain in man forever, since he is flesh." Somehow the vital spirit in each of us is God's spirit. Somehow at each person's conception in the womb God breathes into flesh the pulsing breath of life. He does this in a hidden way, through the activity of the husband and wife. After the flood God does not simply start repopulating the wide open earth. He tells Noah and his wife to do it. "Be fruitful and multiply and fill the earth."

Today with all the talk about over-population some people may think that this command has been carried out too well. There are people, it seems, who are sincerely convinced that the earth is really too crowded for decent human life or is on the verge of becoming so. And they are working with might and brain to decrease the fertility of the human womb. All this despite the curious fact that a big majority of human beings, instead of showing signs of panic because of the press of others hemming them in, rather choose to live in the most crowded places which we call cities. Whatever the problem really is—overpopulation or maldistribution of people and goods—it is a fact that there are many other people whose attitude reflects the mind of the author of Genesis. To them the privilege of fertility is an endless wonder. The living child who is the fruit of their love for one another is to them a source of repeated joy.

The child, long before he realizes it, can be more than a source of simple human joy to his parents. The child can be for them a sign of God's presence and therefore a source of high contemplation and of rejoicing in God. The Old Testament's book of Wisdom says, "From the greatness and beauty of created things their original author, by analogy, is seen." You don't have to be alone under the stars or at the foot of snow-topped Alps or on the rim of the Grand Canyon in order to see God in created things. All you have to do is look into the face of a child. The greatness and beauty of stars and mountains and rivers cannot compare with the greatness and beauty of a child, because a child is a person and God's image in flesh. Children can exasperate you at times and test your patience to the breaking point— just as you and I did when we were children. But as you don't let this keep you from loving them, so you needn't let it keep you from seeing them for what they really are— the fruit of God's fertile love as well as yours, and signs of God's presence in your home.

If an insight such as this becomes more clearly focused in our minds as a result of reading the flood story in Genesis, we can perhaps do without quick and complete answers to some of the questions that the reading raises for us. Rainbows can still be seen; and men and women, like Noah and his wife, are still blessed by God when they increase and multiply and fill the earth.

Chapter 3

Happy Believers

ABRAHAM and SARAH (Genesis 12-25)

TODAY in a mosque at Hebron in southwestern Jordan, Arab Moslems pray to God at the tombs of Abraham and Sarah. These two have been dear to the memory of Jews, Christians, and Moslems for centuries. The Roman martyrology, which is the Catholic Church's official book of saints, lists Saint Abraham on October 9 as the father of all believers. Saint Paul in the 4th chapter of his letter to the Romans argues that Abraham is not only the flesh and blood father of the Jewish people but also the spiritual father of all those who have faith in God.

God teaches us by the lives of men and women who have been key figures in his work of blessing the human race. Such were Abraham and Sarah. Some of Abraham's ways will leave you justifiably shocked. In chapter 12 of Genesis you will read how he showed cool contempt for his wife Sarah and a heartless unconcern for her sexual integrity. He told the Egyptians that she was his sister in order to keep them from knowing that she was his wife. Well aware of her striking beauty, Abraham felt sure that some Egyptian would demand her for a wife even if this meant the necessity of getting rid of her husband. Better to pass her off as his sister; that way they could have her and do what they wanted with her, but his precious neck would not be harmed. We may well wonder also at Sarah's reaction to this insult; apparently she didn't even see the affair as an insult, but went right along with it without any resentment against her cautious husband.

Then too, Abraham had other wives besides Sarah. This is a problem we meet often in the Old Testament. A little careful thought shows that polygamy inflicts serious injustice on at least some of the wives and on the children of the polygamist. It seems that Abraham, and many another Old Testament saint after him, was unaware of the injustice involved in his polygamy. He failed to rise above the centuries of custom that had made this an accepted practice in his Babylonian homeland. And God, whose wisdom in dealing with men is infinitely patient, did not forbid Abraham to follow this long-standing custom of his ancestors. It was better in the long run for the Hebrews to find out for themselves how this practice of polygamy degraded the human person, especially women, and brought misery to families and to nations. Thus experienced in the evils of polygamy the human family would be in a good position to appreciate what Jesus Christ did for marriage.

So Saint Abraham proved himself more than a little selfish and cowardly, and he appears to have been sunk in ignorance about the evils of polygamy. But God took this very earthy man and made him, along with his favorite wife, key instruments in his plan to save the human family. This plan reached its high point in the person of one of Abraham's descendants, Jesus. The opening words of Matthew's gospel call him the son of Abraham.

It was in fact Abraham's faith in God's promise to bless the world through a son of his by Sarah that made him a saint in spite of his limitations. God's promise that Abraham would father a son by Sarah is presented by Genesis as humanly unbelievable because of the fact that childless Sarah was long past the time of child-bearing. His first reaction to God's promise was spontaneous laughter. "And as Abraham fell prostrate, he laughed and said to himself, Shall a son be born to one who is hundred years old? Shall Sarah who is ninety bear a child?"

Later, when Abraham was told the same incredible thing again by God's messengers, Sarah laughed too. This was the quick laughter that sprang from the hearts of two good people who were faced with the human impossibility of God's promise. Later, with Sarah's baby on the way, both of them had sobered up considerably and were overwhelmed with the realization that human impossibility does not even cause a little difficulty when God is about to act. "Is anything too wonderful for the Lord?" Then their laughter became deep joy over God's loving goodness in giving them a son. "Sarah said, God has given me cause for laughter, and whoever hears of it will laugh with me."

After all the laughing it was fitting to name the little boy Isaac, which is a Hebrew word meaning "he laughs." At his birth, and at a critical event in his childhood, the faith of Abraham and Sarah was strengthened to a point where it could and did make them saints.

The crisis of Isaac's childhood is told in the 22nd chapter of Genesis. It is a passage that can be very disturbing to modern readers. Genesis says that Abraham was commanded by God to kill his son Isaac as a sacrificial victim. Abraham is in the process of offering this sacrifice when at the last minute he is stopped by an angel of God and told to offer up a ram instead. What does all this mean? How did the old man know that it was really God who was telling him to kill his son? And how did he know at the end that it was really God's angel telling him to act contrary to the original command? If we try to put ourselves in Abraham's place and imagine what sort of assurances we would have demanded that the killing of Isaac really was, and then was not, God's will, we will begin to see how strange the story is. Abraham apparently made no such demands. This uncritical attitude, in a man who loved his son dearly, perhaps indicates that we are not dealing here with a clear-cut divine command given and then withdrawn, but rather with a psychological development within Abraham.

We know from the Bible as well as from other sources that child sacrifice was practiced by the people of Abraham's world. He saw others from time to time offering up their children as slain sacrificial victims to their gods. What can we expect from a man so strongly influenced by his neighbors as Abraham was except that he too would get the idea of sacrificing his son to God? While we rightly condemn child sacrifice as something horrible, we might briefly acknowledge that the sentiment which prompted it—misguided as this sentiment was—had something splendid about it. Nothing was too good, not even a precious son like Isaac, to give to God! The terrible error lay in the fact that this giving of a dear son to God was thought to mean that the son should be killed. Did Abraham reach this state of mind and did he interpret his compulsion to sacrifice Isaac as a sign of God's will? And was the angel that stopped him his own conscience better informed through deeper thought and finally seeing that his plan to kill Isaac was really not God's will?

Such an explanation of Genesis 22 may labor under as many difficulties as the ordinary one. It is a text that must be wrestled with! And in any case it shows us Abraham shaken by an experience that stretched his faith to the point of heroic sanctity. And Sarah, if we can judge from other events in their lives, was not far behind him.

Chapter 4

Not Enough Courage

LOT and WIFE   (Genesis 19)

L OT was one man in a vast stream of people on the move
from lower Mesopotamia towards the northwest in the
19th century B.C. With his grandfather Terah he went from
Ur up the Tigris-Euphrates valley to Haran. Then after his
grandfather's death in Haran he moved on south with his
uncle Abraham into Canaan, a land that was later to be
called Palestine.

Abraham and Lot were nomad shepherds there in Palestine, and both of them soon became very wealthy. In order
to avoid arguments over grazing land they agreed to live
and move apart. Abraham ranged the hill country west of
the Jordan river while Lot took his flocks and family into
the river basin.

Although they lived apart Abraham and Lot remembered
that they were blood relatives, and Abraham especially felt
responsible for his nephew. This loyalty of Abraham is
brought out dramatically in the 14th chapter of Genesis
where we are told that four tribal chiefs raided Sodom,
the city where Lot had settled. Lot's whole family along
with all their movable property was carried north of Damas-
cus. When Abraham learned of this raid and of the fact
that Lot and his family were prisoners, he organized his

own pursuit party of 318 men and rescued Lot and his family along with their goods. So they took up residence again at Sodom.

Genesis tells us that there was a great deal wrong at Sodom, and it singles out homosexuality (Sodomy) as a practice calling for special blame. Abraham, knowing that his nephew lived in Sodom and convinced that God was about to destroy the city, used all his powers of persuasion in a prayer asking God to spare the people who lived there. God spared Lot and some of his family, but the city was destroyed.

The disaster came quick and irresistible. One day two strangers came into Sodom, and Lot invited them to stay at his house. At first they told him they planned to spend the night outdoors, but when he pressed them they accepted his kind invitation and followed him to his home where a meal was served. Just as they were all getting ready to go to bed for the night, shouts were heard from the outside. A mob of Sodomites were yelling for Lot to give them his two guests to abuse. In his efforts to talk some sense into their heated minds, Lot went so far as to offer them his own two daughters to use as they might please if they would agree not to violate his guests. This bargain shocks us; sometimes the oriental law of hospitality went to fantastic extremes. Like many another mob, this one refused to listen to Lot and started to push him out of their way so that they could break into his house to get at the strangers. But Lot's two guests quickly pulled him back inside and somehow kept the mob outside.

Inside the house Lot's guests told him that he and his family must leave the city at once if they wished to escape the general destruction that was hanging over it. Lot's sons-in-law thought he was joking when he gave them this urgent message; and they decided to disregard it. When

Lot himself hesitated, the stranger hurried him along, with his wife and two daughters, out of the city and away from it to a little place called Segor. At dawn the destruction came. "The sun had risen on the earth when Lot entered Segor. The LORD poured down on Sodom and Gomorra sulphur and fire from the LORD out of heaven. He overthrew those cities and the whole region, all the inhabitants of the cities and the plants of the soil." Abraham too was watching from a distance and he saw the smoke of Sodom's burning.

At the last minute Lot's family had escaped—all but one of its members. Lot's wife had stopped to look back longingly at her home there in Sodom, hating to leave it, hoping the destruction would not be complete and wishing for a quick return. The burning stuff caught her where she stood and her life was gone. Later the spot was seen to be encrusted with salt, and so the story went around that Lot's wife had been changed into salt.

Lot and his two daughters lived in a cave high up in the hills. Neither of Lot's daughters had borne a child. There in the cave they gave up hope of ever finding husbands to replace the two who lay buried beneath the ruins of Sodom. So great was their desire for children that they made their father drunk and then slept with him until each conceived a child. This is the last we hear of Lot and his family.

Lot didn't go along with the ways of his fellow Sodomites, and they ridiculed him for daring to tell them they were doing wrong. He was a good man; but in Sodom the good men were too far outnumbered to accomplish much. Even in Lot's own family there was uncertainty about who could be depended on. The fact that his wife was killed for looking back the way she did is an indication that her mind was not firmly set against the sins of the people of Sodom. Would the story have been different if she had been more of a support to her husband? God had told Abraham that if ten good people could be found in Sodom the city would be spared. Lot's family would have made six!

Christian husbands and wives today, reflecting on this raw story of Lot's family, will ask themselves some questions. Are we, as a family, living according to the teachings of Christ? Or are we, even in matters where a firm stand on Christian principle is urgently called for—such as the personal dignity and rights of every human being—indistinguishable from those who are not even claiming to be living by Christian motives? Are we conscious of our vocation to bear witness to the reality of Christ and his saving work in the world today, and to be the yeast of his parable which influences the whole batch of dough?

A family united in its worship of God and in its obedience to his law will without making any show of it exert a strong influence for good on all who come in contact with its members. Jesus said, "Let your light shine before men and they will see your good action and praise your Father who is in heaven."

Chapter 5

Welcome Stranger

BETHUEL and WIFE (Genesis 24)

OLD Abraham was anxious about finding a wife for his favorite son Isaac. A Hebrew father nineteen centuries before Christ had a great deal more to say than a modern father about the choice of a bride for his son. Abraham was worried about the problem of preserving in his family the worshipping of the one true God. And in his judgment a girl from one of the polytheistic families among whom he lived would not be a suitable wife for Isaac.

So Abraham sent his servant north to the country where he himself had once lived, in upper Mesopotamia, to find a bride for Isaac in one of the families related to them by blood. After a long trip the man came to a stop one evening at the public well outside the city of Nabor.

Women were coming and going at the well. While Abraham's servant was standing there, a lovely girl came out to the well and filled her pitcher with water. The servant ran up to her and asked her for a drink. She gladly gave it and said. "I will draw water also for your camels until they have finished drinking."

While the girl was watering his camels, the man kept looking at her. He was pleased, because her act of kindness to him and to his animals was the very thing that he had just decided on in his own mind as the sign by which he would recognize the girl whom God intended as the bride for his master's son. He put a gold ring in her nose (another custom slightly different from our own!) and two gold bracelets on her wrists. Then he learned that she was Rebecca, and that her father was Abraham's nephew, Bethuel. He asked her if there was room in her house for him to spend the night. She told him they had plenty of food also for the animals and lots of room.

While the old servant was thanking God for all this, Rebecca ran on home to tell her parents and her brother Laban about their visitor from the south. Laban ran out to meet him, welcomed him to their home, and took care of his camels.

Before starting to eat with them, Abraham's servant said he had something important to tell them. He told them who he was and why he had come and what had happened at the well to convince him that Rebecca was the girl he was looking for. Rebecca's family was quick to see the will of God in all this and said, "Here before you is Rebecca; take her and go. Let her be married to your master's son as the LORD has decided."

Again the servant thanked God for the way his business was turning out. Then he gave costly presents to Rebecca and to her mother. He had dinner with them and slept in their home.

Next morning Abraham's servant was eager to get out on the road home; but Rebecca's family was not so eager to see her go. They asked the man to stay for a while. When he said no to this invitation, they called Rebecca to ask her if she was willing to go right away. She said, "I will." So they made no further objection, but blessed her, "May you, sister become a thousand times ten thousand, and may your descendants conquer the gates of their foes."

So Bethuel and his wife and their son Laban saw Rebecca off to the south country where she was to become the wife of Isaac, the mother of twins Esau and Jacob, one of the famous grandmothers of the Hebrew people and of Jesus.

When we read this 24th chapter of the book of Genesis, the spontaneous welcome which met Abraham's servant in the home of Bethuel looks as refreshing as the cool water from Rebecca's pitcher. The Hebrews of the Old Testament times were famous for their hospitality; what they owned they considered as belonging in some way to the stranger who happened to visit them.

Our Christian vocation, far from relieving us of this obligation to welcome other people into our lives, deepens it and gives it a new and stronger motive. We have been alerted to the fact that at the last judgment Christ will say to those on his right, "Come, you blessed ones of my Father. Receive as your inheritance the kingdom which was prepared for you from the founding of the world. For I was hungry and you gave me something to eat. I was thirsty and you gave me something to drink. I was a stranger and you welcomed me into your midst." The new motive for opening our minds and hearts and ears to other people is the fact that Jesus Christ has identified himself with them. "I tell you, as long as you did it for one of these least brothers of mine, you did it for me."

The practice of welcoming others into our lives should not be limited to those fairly rare occasions when we meet perfect strangers who need our help. Within the Christian home each member of the family can learn to be attentive to the needs of all the others and to be generous with his time and his energy for their sake. Such a spirit of welcome within the family will not be confined there but will spread to the larger family in which the very least person is the brother of Christ.

God still speaks to us through the family of Rebecca, because the record of the family's warm welcome to Abraham's servant is there in God's book for us to read. And Jesus said, "Blessed are those who hear the word of God and keep it."

Chapter 6

God's Guiding Hand

ISAAC and REBECCA   (Genesis 24-35)

Today at a Catholic wedding Mass the priest asks God to make the bride kneeling at the altar to be like Rebecca of the Old Testament. The book of Genesis, beginning in chapter 24, tells about her marriage to Abraham's son Isaac.

In the 18th century B.C. Hebrew parents often arranged the marriages of their sons and daughters. So we find old Abraham deciding that son Isaac is not going to marry a native Canaanite girl but rather one from a group of Abraham's own relatives who live farther north. Abraham had no definite girl in mind when he sent his servant to find her.

When the servant arrived at the place where his master's kin lived, he set up what seems a curious standard to use in picking a wife for Isaac. While he was standing at a water spring watching the young women of the city coming out to draw water, he prayed to God and said, "Now if I say to a young woman, Lower your jar that I may drink, and she answers, Drink, and I will also water your camels, she it is whom you have chosen for your servant Isaac."

One of the girls did this, a girl named Rebecca who turned out to be Abraham's grand-niece. Although the only quality Abraham's servant seemed to demand ahead of time was that the girl should have a generous spirit—giving him a drink and offering to water his camels—she was in fact beautiful and lively and even more generous than he expected. She invited him into her home. "We have plenty of straw and fodder, and there is room to spend the night."

Inside the house as they were about to eat, Abraham's servant made his proposal. Would Rebecca's parents, and Rebecca herself, agree that she would become the bride of Isaac whom neither they nor she had ever seen? When the servant told them how he had felt the hand of God in the whole affair up to that point, they decided he was right. Next day when Rebecca's parents wanted her to stay on with them for a few days before moving south to her new life, she was the one who decided there should be no delay. So they blessed her good-bye and wished her an immense fertility. "May you, sister, become a thousand times ten thousand." Hebrew society of those days had its problems; but over-population was not one of them!

So Rebecca became Isaac's bride. He had been grieving over the death of his mother, and a touching remark of Genesis shows how much Rebecca meant to her husband. "Isaac led Rebecca into the tent and took her to wife. Because he loved her, Isaac was consoled for the loss of his mother." Twins were born to them, Esau and Jacob. Even though Isaac and Rebecca were thrilled to have these children after a rather long period during which it seemed that she would never bear a child, trouble developed between the two boys and increased when their parents took sides—Isaac preferring Esau and Rebecca giving her special love to Jacob. Especially painful to both parents, for reasons not explained in Genesis, were the non-Hebrew wives of son Esau.

When Isaac was old and nearly blind, an incident occurred which shook him badly and brought new anxiety into his family. In Hebrew families of that day a great deal of importance was attached to inheritance rights. The first born son was supposed to get the lion's share of his father's property. Old Isaac decided it was time to declare officially that Esau, who had been born a few seconds before his twin brother Jacob, was to have his father's blessing and be put in a position to inherit his property. So he told Esau to go and shoot a head of his favorite game animal and to prepare a meal for the occasion.

While Esau was out hunting, Jacob at his mother's bidding deceived his father into thinking he was Esau and won from him the blessing of the first born son which belonged to his brother. When Esau came back with his father's favorite dish prepared, Isaac was deeply disturbed by the trick his other son had played on him. But because he considered his spoken word irrevocable once it was out of his mouth, Isaac decided there was nothing he or anyone else could do to change the situation. Jacob was now in the position of first born son and that was that.

But Esau decided that something could be done. He gave chase with murder in his eye and Jacob went north. By the time he came back several years later, Esau's anger had cooled and they were able to live together as brothers. But for a while it looked as if blood was going to be shed within that family circle. Little else is said in Genesis about Isaac and Rebecca except the notice of death and burial.

The book of Genesis tells about these two people not only to preserve a family history, but also to show that God's purpose was being accomplished in their lives. Their belonging to each other as man and wife is seen by Abraham's servant and Rebecca's parents as the will of God. The birth of their children was God's answer to Isaac's prayer. The blessing he wished on his son Jacob in view of marriage shows how deeply aware of God this old man was. "May

God Almighty bless you and make you fruitful; may he multiply you so that you may become many nations."

In the mixture of joy and sorrow that their lives turned out to be, Isaac and Rebecca believed that God was interested in them and that he was directing the events—pleasant and painful—of their married life. There are men and women like them who believe the same thing today. The priest's prayer at the wedding Mass is often answered.

Chapter 7

Love for Children

JACOB and RACHEL (Genesis 25-50)

To the right of the road leading into Bethlehem from the north you can see a white round-roofed shrine built over a woman's grave. Her name was Rachel, favorite wife of the patriarch Jacob; their family history is told in the last half of the book of Genesis, beginning with chapter 25.

Rachel died near Bethlehem while giving birth to her second son Benjamin. Jacob, who was a nomad shepherd, buried her there before moving on. Awareness of Rachel's tomb lay deep in the minds of the Jews. In the 6th century B.C. the prophet Jeremiah described the grief of Judean mothers over their deported sons by saying that Rachel was crying for her children who were gone. And in the New Testament's gospel of Saint Matthew the mothers of King Herod's victims are still being represented by Rachel. "A voice was heard in Rama, weeping and much wailing, Rachel weeping over her children; and she would not be comforted, because they are not alive."

Does the life story of Jacob's family have any meaning for Christian husbands and wives today? Jacob practiced polygamy and seems to have been as unaware of its evils as his grandfather Abraham. Nor was he above telling a lie when it was profitable. But as you read the story of

Jacob and Rachel you will begin to see through their faults to the true greatness of their minds and hearts. For one thing, you will be struck by their deep love for their children and by the ways in which they showed this love.

For some time Rachel was unable to bear Jacob a child, and this was a cause of keen sorrow to her. Chapter 30 of Genesis describes her problem. "When Rachel saw that she was not bearing children to Jacob, she became jealous of her sister (this was Lia who had already given Jacob four sons) and said to Jacob, Give me children or I shall die. Jacob became impatient with Rachel and answered her, Can I take the place of God, who has made you barren?" How jubilant she was when some time later she did bear Jacob a son, Joseph. Her only wish was that she would be able to repeat the performance. "May the Lord give me another son." She did bear another son, as we have seen, and she died to give him birth.

Not only Rachel's but also Jacob's love for children can be seen on many a page of Genesis. In chapter 33 when Jacob's brother Esau urges him to speed his pace on a journey, Jacob protested that this would overtax the strength of his children. "My lord (so he addresses his brother Esau) can see that the children are young, and the flocks and herds giving suck are a care to me; if overdriven for a single day, the whole flock will die. Let my lord go on ahead of his servant and I shall proceed slowly at the pace of the stock I am driving and at the pace of the children, until I come to my lord at Seir." Jacob knew how to feel with his children and even with his sheep and goats and to take their tender needs into his heart. Across many centuries a great-grandson of his would say, "I am the good shepherd, and I know my sheep and they know me."

Jealous rivalry among Jacob's sons brought serious trouble into his family. Jacob himself was partly the cause of this jealousy. The first son Rachel had given him, Joseph, was his father's favorite—and Jacob seems to have made no effort to conceal his preference. And Genesis shows Joseph as a boy inclined to side with his father against his brothers. So when an opportunity came their way Joseph's brothers, who almost decided to kill their brother, sold him as a slave into Egypt and reported to their father that his favorite son had been killed by a wild animal. Jacob believed them when they showed him the blood-splashed coat that Joseph had worn and he was inconsolable. "I will go down mourning, to my son in the nether world. So his father wept over him."

Later on, when it became necessary for Jacob to part with his youngest son Benjamin, he was again completely broken up. "You know that my wife bore me two sons; one is gone from me, and I said: He has surely been torn to pieces; I have not seen him since. If you take this one also from me, and some harm befalls him, you will bring down my gray hairs with sorrow to the grave."

After years of trouble in his family, long after Rachel's death and Joseph's disappearance, Jacob went to Egpyt and found his long lost son still alive. Chapter 46 moves with the happy excitement of their meeting. "When he met him he fell on his neck, weeping long in his arms. Israel (Jacob's other name) said to Joseph, Now I can die, after seeing you still alive."

Still later, Old Jacob is filled with joy over his grandchildren. Genesis tells what happened when Jacob met Joseph's two sons. "Joseph brought them near him, and he kissed and embraced them. Then Israel said to Joseph, I had no hope of ever seeing you, and now God has allowed me to see your children as well." It comes as no surprise to read a little farther on that when Jacob was dying his most devoted son "fell on his father's face, weeping over him and kissing him."

These few examples from the life of Jacob and Rachel show how warm was the love they had for their children and with what moving affection they expressed it. Loving affection is not weak sentimentality. If it were, we would never be reading in the gospel of Saint Mark that Christ blessed the children by embracing them; they could feel his love in the touch of his hands.

What a blessing it is for children to grow up in a home where they are made to feel that they are loved and wanted. What a joy for them to know that they are being treated, in spite of their immaturity and frequent nerve-scraping antics, like persons and not just objects. How good it is for children to know that father has time for their vast little world of toy trains and picture books, time to answer their struggling little questions. And how wonderful to feel the warmth of mother's love in a good-night hug and to give her the same with a kiss.

It isn't easy to love generously and to be perfect in showing one's love outwardly. Part of the bitterness of Joseph's brothers was the result of their feeling that their father was not giving them the attention they wanted. Jacob's problem was not that he showed too much love for Joseph but rather that he didn't show enough love for his other sons. We won't be perfect in loving either. But, as G.K. Chesterton said, if a thing is worth doing, it is worth doing badly!

Chapter 8

God's Strange Way

JUDAH and TAMAR   (Genesis 38)

A T first glance the affair between Judah and Tamar as told in the 38th chapter of Genesis seems to offer nothing in a constructive way for the thinking of husbands and wives today. But a closer look may uncover an important lesson.

The Bible is frank about these two. Tamar, twice a widow and childless, wanted a baby of her own so badly that she was willing to do anything to get one. Her father-in-law Judah, whose wife had died, went and served himself to a prostitute who happened to be, without his knowing it, Tamar herself. By this union she conceived and gave birth to twin boys, Pares and Zarah.

Tamar was not the only woman whose longing for motherhood or pleasure or money has led to such a course of action. Judah was not the only male who has surrendered to the power of uncontrolled passion. They are not unique, not even greatly remarkable, in their sin. Nor is Tamar unusual as a female victim to male hypocrisy when Judah showed himself ready to put her to death for being pregnant. Certainly Judah's change of heart on this point, when he was presented with unanswerable proof that he was the father of her child, will strike nobody as heroic. Still, there is something wonderful about these two—so God seems to have thought.

In chapter 55 of his book the prophet Isaiah says, "My thoughts are not your thoughts, nor are your ways my ways, says the Lord. As high as the heavens are above the earth, so high are my ways above your ways and my thoughts above your thoughts." We begin to see how these ways of God worked in the pathetic story of Judah and Tamar when we open the New Testament and read on its first page that one of Jesus' ancestors was a man named Pares. The first gospel goes out of its way to mention the origin of this great-grandfather of Jesus seventeen centuries removed. He specifies that Pares was one of the twins born to Tamar after she had played prostitute for her father-in-law, Judah.

Because of Tamar's decision to have herself a child no matter how and because of Judah's unknowing patronage of her prostitution, Jesus Christ belongs to the tribe of Judah. Because of the fruit of Judah's sinful union with Tamar, the Catholic Church sings on September 8, birthday of the Virgin Mary: "Mary is brilliant with royal ancestry, sprung from the famous stock of David, of the tribe of Judah." Judah had, besides his two deceased sons Her and Onan and his illegitimate sons Pares and Zarah, a legitimate son named Shelah. But it is not through Shelah that the Bible links the Virgin Mary and her son Jesus to the tribe of Judah. The link is Pares, Judah's illegitimate son by his daughter-in-law. To Pares and through him to his parents God gave the privilege of being the source of the Messiah's blood. We may well ask why the writer of Genesis decided to preserve this unflattering story of the patriarch Judah and why God inspired him to make it a part of the Bible. Or why the first gospel of the New Testament departs from standard procedure, when it gives a family tree for Christ, by mentioning four women in that family tree—including Judah's daughter-in-law. He who was to be known and loved as the friend of sinners was not ashamed to have some of them in his family roots. "My thoughts are not your thoughts, nor are your ways my ways, says the Lord."

God's favor to Pares and to his parents cannot, of course, be taken to mean that he approved of what they did. But it does mean that God is powerful enough to accomplish wonders even in the lives of people who are unworthy of such wonders. God's way with Pares shows that the Creator, who knows how to bring light out of darkness every morning when he makes his sun to shine, knows also how to bring order out of disordered human lives, blessing out of tragedy, good out of evil. This is the lesson we can learn from the affair of Judah and Tamar in Genesis. Our way is to lose heart over the disorder, despair over the tragedy, or go to pieces over the evil, in our lives. God's way, as it is made known to us in the story of Judah and Tamar, is to turn the evil, the tragedy, the disorder, to the service of his wisdom. Our need to learn this way of God may be the reason why the story was included in the Bible.

With the New Testament teaching to help us see more clearly, we can be aware of the fact that the biggest evil in our lives is our disobedience to God, our sin. The New Testament, even more than the Old, can also help us to see that God is powerful and wise enough to bring good even out of this evil which is our sin. Saint Paul was turning this truth over and over in his mind when he wrote in the 11th chapter of his letter to the Romans, "Oh the depth of God's rich wisdom and knowledge. How unsearchable are his judgments and untrackable his ways!" God's way of drawing good from evil—as well as his endless mercy—is the reason why our sorrow for sin should be penetrated with joy.

Then too, knowing how patient God is in dealing with us,

knowing his respect for the shabbiest of us, knowing his way of bringing good out of evil—this will help us to imitate him as Christ said we must do. It will help us to put up with one another's faults and weaknesses. It will help us to see that God has a purpose in not preventing those weaknesses. Without condoning moral disorders in ourselves or in others, we can learn to be patient while we try to correct them. Discouragement over sin is a state of mind that does not fit God's love and does not reflect an awareness of his strange ways.

The story of Judah and Tamar in Genesis teaches us, not so much by what they did as by God's great wisdom in bringing good out of the tangle of their lives. As we read about them we must keep in mind that God has not changed; he can do the same with the evil, big or not quite so big, in our lives. This is not a false optimism but a true one, based not on wishful thinking but on the truth which God has revealed about himself in the Bible.

Chapter 9

Faithful Husband

JOSEPH and ASENATH   (Genesis 30-50)

I N the 17th century B.C. a caravan moved southwest from Dothan in Palestine to Egypt. With it was a slave boy named Joseph, son of the Hebrew patriarch Jacob. When you read the story of Joseph's stormy life in chapters 30 to 50 of Genesis, you will learn to love this best of Jacob's sons.

As a last minute alternative to killing him, Joseph's envious brothers sold him as a slave. He was mourned as dead by his father, who believed their trumped up story that Joseph had been killed by a wild animal. Joseph was to pass many a long year in Egypt before Jacob's troubled family would come together again.

God teaches us not only by the words of the Bible but also by the very events in the lives of men like Joseph. Joseph's trust in God at a time of severe danger to his life, his patience when his good name was smeared, his big-hearted forgiveness and affection for his humbled brothers, his loving attention to his aging father—all this makes him a pattern for us.

We also notice that Joseph was a family man, a husband and father, even though the book of Genesis says only a little about this side of his life. Chapter 41 gives the brief notice of his marriage to an Egyptian girl named Asenath.

45

Two sons were born to them, Menassheh and Ephraim. The same brief statement is repeated in chapter 46. Add to this the blessing pronounced by Jacob over his two grandsons in chapter 48, and you have all that we can know about the family life of Joseph.

But something happened before his marriage that shows us what kind of husband he was to be. Chapter 39 of Genesis tells us that Joseph was a trusted slave in the home of his Egyptian owner, Potiphar. The Bible, always plain in such matters, tells us that Potiphar's wife was struck by the young slave's handsome features and asked him to share a bed with her. Joseph's answer was not slow in coming. "Because of me, my master is not concerned about anything in the house, but has put all that he owns in my care. He exercises no greater authority in this house than I, nor has he withheld a single thing from me, except yourself, because you are his wife. How then can I commit this great crime, and sin against God?" But she would not listen to him and kept trying to get him to do what she wanted. When she saw that he would not change his mind, her longing turned to spite and she accused Joseph to her husband of trying to seduce her—and Joseph was thrown in jail.

Joseph's victory over this kind of temptation can inspire husbands today. Sometimes they are faced with situations like his. Joseph's motives for refusing to yield to the demands of Potiphar's wife, far from seeming out of date or unrelated to real life, will be recognized as the same strong motives that make husbands faithful to their wives today. Notice Joseph's earnest words to the woman—You are his wife. To have done what she wanted would have been, in Joseph's mind, a deed of enormous injustice to her husband. It would also have been an attack, not less brutal just because she invited it, on her dignity as a wife. Worst of all, in Joseph's assessment of the situation, it would have been a slap in the face of God, the Author of marriage. "How then can I commit this great crime, and sin against God?"

These motives for keeping one's promise of fidelity in marriage should be even more powerful for Christian husbands than they were for God's people in the Old Testament. Christ made marriage into a sacrament; that is, into a sacred sign of his own loving union with all believers and a source of supernatural life in his Church. Marriage therefore and the use of sex is something sacred, like water for Baptism and bread and wine for the Eucharist. For this reason it is not only a sin against justice to one's mate but also a sacrilege—the profanation of a sacrament—when a husband seeks sexual gratification in anyone else besides his wife.

And the wife, she must learn well her part in keeping her husband faithful to herself and to God. She will pray often for her husband and for her marriage, and she will rely on God who joined them to keep them all that they ought to be. She will not neglect to keep herself attractive in her husband's eyes. She will continue through her thirties and forties and beyond, to give herself with generous love to the man who married her because she meant so much to him. She will not deceive herself into thinking that she is doing the will of God and becoming more spiritual by playing down the sexual side of her married life—or even by refusing the debt which she owes to her husband and making him think of the possibility of finding the equivalent elsewhere.

Saint Paul in the 7th chapter of his first letter to the Corinthians is firm on this point. "Let the husband pay the debt to his wife. By the same token let the wife pay the debt to her husband. For the wife does not have the right over her own body; rather, the husband has. By the same token again, the husband does not have the right over his own body; rather the wife has. Do not deny one another these rights, except maybe by mutual agreement, for a time, in order to have leisure for prayer before coming back together again." These words of Saint Paul make it clear that, in his judgment, the husband and the wife are each very much responsible for the fidelity of the other.

To be a faithful husband—or a faithul wife—is not the easiest thing in the world. Occasions for infidelity are plentiful. More than once in a lifetime great strength of character, along with a ready desire for God's help, is needed. More than one victory will come only at the cost of personal pain and sacrifice. Joseph's victory landed him in jail; but the victory was well worth the price. So is ours today.

Chapter 10

God Acts Through Men

AMRAM and YOKEBED   (Exodus 1-2)

THE parents of Moses were eclipsed in the memory of the Hebrews by their great son. Even so, not only their names, but also a few precious facts about them have been preserved for us in the Old Testament's book of Exodus.

Exodus, which is the Bible's second book, opens with a description of hard times for the Hebrews in Egypt. Gone was the happy freedom of Hebrew shepherds on the grassland of Goshen in the eastern half of the Nile's delta. The Hebrews, foreigners in Egypt, had been reduced to slaves, and they were groaning under an unbearable burden of drudgery for one of Egypt's Pharaohs. Worse still, a systematic movement had been started by the Egyptian ruler to stop the natural increase of the Hebrew male population; boy babies were to be killed.

Chapter 2 of Exodus begins with a hurried statement about the marriage of a Hebrew couple and about the conception and birth of their son. Their names, Amram and Yokebed, are given later on, in chapter 6. Both were descendants of Levi, who was the patriarch Jacob's third son. By Egyptian law the life of their baby boy was illegal. But Yokebed, the mother, managed to keep him hidden for three months. When danger mounted, her love for the child invented a plan to save his life. She made a water-proof basket, put the little one in it, and set it afloat on the Nile River at a place where the water was calm and where, she knew, Pharaoh's daughter often came to bathe herself.

The ruse worked. "Pharaoh's daughter," says Exodus, "came down to the river to bathe, while her maids walked along the river bank. Noticing the basket among the reeds, she sent her handmaid to fetch it. On opening it, she looked, and lo, there was a baby boy, crying! She was moved with pity for him and said, 'It is one the Hebrews' children.' " Then the little boy's sister, who had stationed herself nearby, came up to ask if she should go and get a Hebrew woman to nurse the child. Pharaoh's daughter said, "Yes, do so." Soon the girl returned with her mother, Yokebed, who took her baby and nursed him as she had been doing for the past three months. Now she could lay aside her fear, because she knew that Pharaoh's daughter would see to it that he was allowed to live. Yokebed took the child home and raised him until the woman who had saved his life adopted him as her own son and named him Moses. Later in the book of Exodus we learn that Miriam was the names of Moses' sister and that he had a brother, Aaron.

The gigantic role played by Moses in Israel's history contrasts sharply with these frail beginnings. To his parents' willingness to raise a family in spite of the worst obstacles he owed his conception and birth. His mother's love and resourceful thinking at a time of peril, a small basket floating on the Nile River, his baby voice and the pity it stirred in the heart of an unknown woman, his sister's ready help— these were the things that saved his little life. These were the things through which God, who seemed careless of the danger, saved Moses for his great work as leader of the Hebrew people in their exodus from Egypt.

Amram and Yokebed must have felt in their very bones

the danger that threatened the life of their son. But through it all God was with them, even though they might not have been aware of this. God's love was hidden in Yokebed's love for her child, in her courage and clever planning, in the pitiful little basket afloat on the river, in the little voice of a baby crying and stirring pity in the heart of Pharaoh's daughter, in Miriam's quick eye and ready step.

It should not be hard for Christians to see in such simple human realities as a self-sacrificing father, a loving mother, a much concerned sister, and the sympathy of a stranger, the sign of God's love. These things are taken for granted much of the time, and we are not usually inclined to see anything very deep in them.

But it is clear to us now when we read the book of Exodus that, in the life of Amram and Yokebed and their son Moses, God's mighty love was at work in precisely such ordinary things. Change their names to yours and adjust some of the details to fit your own experience, and you will see that God's loving care for your family is still hidden but discoverable in the self-sacrifice of a father, in the watchful love of a mother, in the ready help of a sister or brother, in the warm heart of a stranger.

Chapter 11

Second Birth

MOSES and SEPPHORA   (Exodus 4)

JORDAN's Mount Nebo looks down into the awesome distance of earth's deepest geological fault, the simmering
valley where the river Jordan plunges into the Dead Sea.
On the other side of the valley, Palestine now partitioned
off to Jordan and Israel, falls away west to the Mediterranean
Sea, north to Lebanon and south to Egypt. Mount Nebo,
described in the last chapter of the Old Testament's book
of Deuteronomy, is the spot where Moses died after feasting
his eager eyes on the promised land across the valley.

From the frail basket holding him afloat on the Nile
to Mount Nebo's lonely summit, Moses had traveled a long
road. Memory of him lived deep and strong in the minds
of his people. The writer of the last chapter of Deuteronomy
spoke for them all when he said, "Since then no prophet has
arisen in Israel like Moses, whom the Lord knew face to
face."

The reader of the books of Exodus, Leviticus, Numbers,
and Deuteronomy, impressed by the massive stature of
Moses as political and religious leader, can easily miss some
unstressed, but not unimportant, sides of the man; for
example, his family life as described in chapters 2 to 4 of
Exodus.

Although his young life had been saved from destruction by an Egyptian princess who later adopted him as her son, Moses never forgot his Hebrew blood. A fugitive from Egypt because he had killed a native for beating up a Hebrew slave, Moses wandered into the desert east of Egypt. There he met and married Sepphora, daughter of a nomadic shepherd named Raguel who was also called Jethro. Moses and Sepphora named their first son Gershom, whom through careless neglect they did not circumcise as the Hebrew law prescribed. Trouble would come from this neglect.

While tending his father-in-law's flock in the mountains of the Sinai peninsula, Moses received God's command to go back to Egypt and to take up the task of liberating his enslaved kinsmen. After complaining about the impossibility of success in this mission, Moses got leave from his father-in-law, packed up his family, and started out. The 4th chapter of Exodus shows us the little group on its way. "So Moses took his wife and his sons, and started back to the land of Egypt, with them riding the ass."

But they were not to have smooth riding all the way. One startling interruption is described in the last part of chapter 4 of Exodus. This description, although it is something of a puzzle to every student of the Bible, can serve us as a stimulant for some worthwhile thought. It reads: "On the journey, at a place where they spent the night the LORD came upon Moses and would have killed him. But Sepphora took a piece of flint and cut off her son's foreskin and, touching his feet, she said, You are a spouse of blood to me. Then God let Moses go. At that time she said, A spouse of blood, in regard to the circumcision."

What does it mean to say that God drew near to Moses and wanted to kill him? How did Sepphora know what was the matter? Who, the boy or Moses, was touched with the cut away foreskin, and why? What do Sepphora's words mean?

Even though a satisfactory answer cannot be given to these questions, the general meaning of the passage is clear. God threatened Mosses with death because he had neglected to have his son circumcised. Moses' wife quickly performed the neglected circumcision, and her husband was allowed to live and to continue on his way to his kinsmen in Egypt.

Chapter 17 of Genesis tells us that Hebrew parents were under a serious obligation to have their sons circumcised. "If any male have not the flesh of his foreskin circumcised, that person shall be cut off from his people." St. Luke tells us in chapter 2 of his gospel that Joseph and Mary saw to the circumcision of the eight-day-old Jesus in keeping with the Jewish law. Moses, on the other hand, who was to threaten the Hebrews with terrible punishment for violations of God's law, himself violated that law by neglecting to have his son circumcised. For this he almost died.

The New Testament, and in particular St. Luke's Acts of the Apostles, makes it clear that Jesus intended the Sacrament of Baptism to take the place of the Old Testament's rite of circumcision. So in place of the obligation imposed on Hebrew parents to have their sons circumcised came the obligation of Christian parents to have their children baptized. As Jesus told Nicodemus, "unless a man is born of water and the Spirit he cannot enter the kingdom of God."

When Christian parents read about Moses and Sepphora in chapter 4 of Exodus they will think of their own religious obligations to their children; chief of these is the obligation to have their children baptized. Conscientious fathers and mothers bring their children in good time to the baptismal font, womb of their new birth as children of the Church. This trip to the parish church with the baby is pretty much taken for granted. But you ought to know what you are doing for your unsuspecting little one. You are taking it to the sacrament which destroys original sin from its soul, fills it with the new life of grace, makes it God's chosen dwelling place, and joins it to the risen body of Christ.

The protective tenderness with which you rightly surround your child on the day of its birth is not as powerful a proof of love as this baptismal visit to your parish church. Nor can you forget that, if you offer your children to God for baptism, you also assume the responsibility of instructing them in the faith. And that instruction, in its turn, will be acceptable only if it carries with it the sincerity of parents whose faith in God and whose mutual respect and love is living proof that their own baptism means as much to them as they expect it to mean to their children.

PART TWO

While the Judges Ruled

Mother of Many

LAPPIDOTH and DEBORAH (Judges 4-5)

LAPPIDOTH, male half of this couple, just gets into the picture by the bare mention of his name. But his wife, the amazing Deborah, held the Hebrew writer's attention for two chapters of the Old Testament's book of Judges.

This seventh book of the Bible, which covers about 150 years of Israel's history just before the Israelite kingdom was formed under Saul, is a story of much violence and bloodshed. God's people had been led by Moses out of Egypt, through the desert, up to to the eastern slope of the Jordan river valley; then by Joshua across the river into Palestine, where they had fought and defeated enough of the native population to gain footholds up and down the land.

But the surviving natives bitterly resented the presence of

the Hebrew invaders; and for years this resentment kept exploding into open war. Besides, the Hebrews were not at peace among themselves. Even though their common blood from Abraham made them kinsmen, they were often locked in bloody feuds. The Bible's story of all this conflict is the book of Judges.

During these troubled times God blessed His people with military leaders, called judges, who were able to fight off Israel's enemies and maintain a fretful peace for short spaces of time. Twelve of these judges are mentioned in the book that is named after them. Best known among them, because their careers are told at greater length, are Gedeon, Jephte, and Samson. Others, like Thola and Elon, get only a few lines of notice. Most surprising of them all is the fourth, whose story is told in chapters 4 and 5; for this judge was a woman, Deborah, wife of Lappidoth.

Chapter 4 tells about Deborah's vital role in a battle fought in north central Palestine between a Hebrew army led by Barac and a native Palestinian army under Sisara's command. Envigorated by Deborah's presence Barac and his men won the battle against superior odds; while Sisara, who thought he had made his escape, was killed in his sleep by a Bedouin woman named Jahel. Chapter 5 which is Deborah's victory song, still rings with the noise of that battle.

The history of God's people in the book of Judges teaches us some lessons that are as vital to us as to them. Practically every episode set down in the book makes it clear that obedience to God's law brings joy into human life while disobedience is paid with misery; that no matter how low men and women may sink morally, God is willing to lift them up again when sorrow for sin drives them to His mercy. But there is, in addition to this, something special that Christian wives can learn from Deborah.

Most women of today will not recognize any similarity

between themselves and Deborah in her position of public authority, or her daring military service, or her passionate victory song after battle. But even though the known details of her life hardly fit the lives of most modern women, there must have been other details, unknown to us, that would make her look much more like her sisters of today. And we do not have to appeal to unknown facts about her to see that she has a meaning for women of all time. She herself gives us the key to this meaning when, in her victory song, she calls herself a mother in Israel.

Deborah was, in her own troubled times, a married woman who took an active interest in her community. More important still, hers was the loving, energetic, life-giving interest of a mother. So her life still speaks to women. Her message is clear; a woman's love must go beyond her home to the larger-than-family community of families in which she lives, and in that larger relationship she must continue to be a mother. The city or country community of which her neighborhood is a part, the schools attended by her children, the hospitals with their sick, the parish of which her family is a unit—all these institutions, and more, have a strong claim on even the busiest homemaker. And since her husband and children, not to mention herself, are deeply involved in these institutions, it should be easy for her to see them as extensions of her home. This means that she must bring a mother' love and understanding into the school, the parish, the neighborhood, into all those relationships that take her out of the four walls of her home.

No need to go into detail on all these possibilities. Let one example, the school, be enough here. The mother with children in school should be personally interested in her children's teachers and classmates and in all that makes up their student life. If she has developed this personal interest she will never admit the idea that her children are exclusively teacher's problem while they are at school. She will rather be persuaded that her child's happy progress in school often depends on sympathetic understanding between parent and teacher. This means that mother must go out of her way to get to know the teacher and so give the teacher a new and very useful way of knowing mother's child. Such communications are all the more necessary now that classrooms are so often over-crowded. In most schools, because of the large enrollment, personal knowledge of each student is difficult for a teacher to acquire. So it is good for mother to call, and even better to call on, the teacher to find out why her youngster got a low arithmetic mark—or to express her surprise at his good conduct mark. Or maybe what is needed is more faithful attendance and active participation in parent-teacher meetings. Whatever form such interest may take in expressing itself, every mother should develop an active, motherly interest in the schools her children attend, because the school is nothing but a necessary extension of her home.

In doing these things you will probably not feel very much like Deborah of Old Testament fame. But you, like Deborah, will be a married woman taking an active interest in your community; and your interest, like hers, will be the life-bearing interest of a mother. If it is unquestionably true that a mother's place is in the home, it is also true that her home is much bigger than her house.

Miracle of Life

MANOAH and WIFE   (Judges 13)

IT is not every day that a baby's conception is announced to the parents ahead of time by an angel. Samson is described in chapter 13 of the Old Testament's book of Judges as one of these distinguished few. This chapter opens with the notice that the Israelites, who had no king as yet, were suffering under the heavy hand of enemy Philistines. God's people lacked a leader; but God was about to supply their need in the person of Samson, son of Manoah.

Manoah was married; but he and his wife had not been blessed with a child. One day a stranger visited Manoah's wife and told her, "Though you are barren and have had no children, yet you will conceive and bear a son." She took this startling bit of news to her husband, who showed an understandably keen interest and wanted to see the stranger for himself. When Manoah's wife received a second visit she ran to get her husband and the two of them listened to the stranger's instructions about the promised child.

Manoah, much impressed, readily believed what he was told and asked the stranger to be his guest at a meal. But the visitor turned down the invitation and suggested that Manoah might, instead, offer a sacrifice to God. When Manoah asked at least to know the stranger's name, he was told, "Why do you ask my name, which is mysterious?"

After these two refusals, Manoah prepared to burn a young goat and some grain in honor of God. As the flame reached upward, the mysterious visitor, to Manoah's bewilderment stepped into the flame and was seen no more. Only then did Manoah realize what his wife had faintly suspected earlier, that the strange messenger was a messenger of God.

Shaken by the experience, Manoah and his wife fell faces down onto the ground and he managed to say, "We will certainly die, for we have seen God." But his wife quieted his fears by assuring him that God would not kill them after making them such a wonderful promise. In due time the child was born and they named him Samson.

Manoah and his wife never saw the angel again. But they did see a great deal of the child for whose sake the angel had visited them. And if the angel's brief visits filled the parents with wonderment, it was little Samson who was the permanent wonder in their life. Although the circumstances of Samson's birth were strange, the birth of a child —which is the greatest wonder described in the 13th chapter of the book of Judges—happens time after time. So often and so uneventfully, in fact, that people can become blind to the miracle that takes place every time a child is born.

A new baby is an awesome thing, man-made and God-made at the same time, squirming proof of a couple's fertile love and of God's dim promise of the boy or girl that will grow into the man or woman that will be: loud-mouthed answer to an unspoken prayer, suckling lover of mother's breast, mystery in whose tiny half-open eyes father sees himself increased and multiplied. An awesome thing indeed!

If it is good for us to think forward to the unknown moment of death, it is also good for us to think back to the unremembered moment when life began in the womb. God himself invites us to do this when he has his sacred writer say in the 7th chapter of the Old Testament's book of Wisdom, "I too am a mortal man, like all the rest, and a descendant of the first man formed of earth. And in my mother's womb I was molded into flesh in a ten-month's period—body and blood, from the seed of man, and the pleasure that accompanies marriage. And I too, when born, inhaled the common air, and fell upon the kindred earth; wailing, I uttered the first sound common to all." The signs of pregnancy are the only outward evidence of the miracle that has taken place in the mother's body, until the miracle itself is born.

The spontaneous sequel to such wholesome reminiscing is an act of thanks and praise to God. The writer of psalm 139 spoke for us all when he said to God, "Truly you have formed my inmost being; you knit me in my mother's womb. I give you thanks that I am fearfully, wonderfully made; wonderful are your works."

In parents this awareness of the miracle of human life should be doubly intense. Not only can they reflect on the marvel of their own origin; they themselves, and God, work the miracle of conception which leads to the miracle which is their child. St. Augustine, early 5th century bishop of Hippo in North Africa, told the people of his diocese, "A dead man arose (he refers to one of the dead whom Jesus called back to life) and men are amazed. So many are born every day, and no one is amazed. If we consider the thing carefully, it is a greater miracle for someone to live who never lived before than for someone who lived once to live again. We see all this, and if His Spirit is in us, all this will be so pleasing to us that we will praise the Maker of it all."

In a world of wonders, parents in whom the wonder of human life begins and grows, should feel very much at home. If they are not aware of this miracle, they do not yet know what they are and what they are doing. They need to learn the lesson taught by Manoah and his wife, who thanked God for the miracle which was Samson. They need the insight of a nurse who said, "I tell you, every time a child is born, it's a miracle."

Chapter 14

Fruits of Violence

SAMSON and WIFE   (Judges 13-16)

L AY people are being urged these days to read the Bible. They are told that familiarity with its pages will deepen their awareness of God whose word it is. Not only the New Testament with its emphasis on the person and teaching of Jesus, but the Old Testament too with its story of the Hebrew people, is said to be an important source of Christian life. This is all to the good.

But while the Bible does sharpen the believer's awareness of God in human life, it also raises some problems in his mind, particularly when he reads the Old Testament. One such problem arises when the reader sees what kind of people God often associated with himself in accomplishing his work. They were not always the best; some of them were not far from being the worst. It may come as something of a shock to learn that God is sometimes unbelievably patient with certain human weaknesses and sins; while at other times he seems to be inhumanly severe. The Bible gives us God not as we might like him to be, but as he is in reality—often puzzling.

Any reader of the Old Testament's book of Judges will agree with what has just been said. And when he comes to the story of Samson in chapters 13 and 16 of the book of

Judges he will know for sure that in Samson God picked up a strange associate indeed.

From chapter 13 the reader can get the impression that Samson was going to be like John the Baptist of the New Testament times. But the rest of the story shows us that there was a vast difference between these two men who were both consecrated to God before they were born.

Samson married a Philistine girl from southwest Palestine against the advice of his parents. On his way to the wedding Samson's extraordinary strength was proved when he had to kill a mountain lion barehanded. At the wedding banquet he had himself a merry time by giving his male attendants a riddle which they could not solve until they learned its answer from Samson's wife. Samson flew into a rage at this and killed thirty Philistines in order to get the wherewithal to pay off his bet; then he left without bothering to take his wife.

Later when he went back to get her, he found her living as the wife of another man, the man who had been best man at his wedding. In reprisal, Samson set fire to the Philistine's grain fields, vineyards, and olive orchards. In their turn the Philistines killed Samson's wife and her family. Samson struck back and killed some of them; then hid out in a cave.

His own fellow Hebrews handed him over to the Philistines; but his unusual strength served him well again, and he escaped after killing a great number of them. Once, in Gaza, he left a harlot's house at midnight to escape a murder plot. Then he fell in love with another Philistine woman, Delilah, who turned out to be his complete undoing by coaxing him to tell her the secret of his strength. He was captured, blinded, and put to slave labor. Finally, while the Philistines were making a fool of him, his strength returned; he wrecked their temple which fell and killed the people in it, including Samson himself. So he died, as violently as he had lived.

St. Paul says that all these things were written for our instruction. What instruction, we wonder, can we get from this story of Samson? You will notice that in spite of Samson's violent and lustful ways he twice prayed to God in his distress. This reminds us that no matter how low a man may sink morally, he should never forget how to ask God to help him.

Not much more can be said about Samson on the constructive side; but we can learn from his mistakes. In practically every event of his life he appears as a violent, headstrong man. And when we read in chapter 14 how his temper flared up over the fact that his nice little riddle had been solved, and how that uncontrolled temper drove him to kill thirty men and abandon his newly wedded wife—we begin to see what a cheap little man he could be, in spite of his enormous strength.

Thinking about Samson's destructive temper may remind us of the times when we ourselves have gotten angry over little things. It is not hard to think of homes that have been broken up—to the irreparable harm of all concerned—by the uncontrolled temper of the man of the house; or of homes that do not break up, but whose members live in more or less constant fear of father's unpredictable explosions. St. Paul's command is as necessary today as when he wrote it: "Husbands, love your wives and do not be bitter toward them." And again, "Fathers, do not irritate your children lest they be dispirited."

Such words would have sounded strange to Samson. But to the conscientious husband and father they hold out a principle that guides his life and helps him to make his house into a home.

Chapter 15

Mother Courage

ELIMELEK and NAOMI   (Ruth)

CROP failure at Bethlehem in southern Palestine forced Elimelek and Naomi to leave their unproductive fields behind and to look for the means of survival somewhere else. With their two sons, Mahelon and Kilion, they went into the tableland of Moab, east of the Dead Sea where they lived for about ten years. The Old Testament's book of Ruth tells their story.

The struggle for food was only one of the problems that plagued this family. While they were living in Moab the head of the family died, leaving Naomi with her two sons, Mahelon and Kilion. Both of them married Moabite women, but died soon afterward, leaving Noami alone.

But the widows of Naomi's sons were very devoted to her and wanted to go with her when she decided to go back to Bethlehem. Naomi, more concerned about the happiness of these two young women than about her own need for their company, tried to talk them out of the idea of going with her. Chapter 1 of the book of Ruth tells what happened. Naomi told them, "Go back, each of you, to your mother's house. May the LORD grant each of you a husband and a home in which you will find rest." But when she kissed them good-by, they insisted on going with her.

It was only after still more pleading that Orpah, Kilion's widow, decided with tears in her eyes that it would be better to stay in her homeland. But Ruth, Mahelon's widow, would not let Naomi go back to Bethlehem alone. "Do not ask me to abandon or forsake you! For wherever you go I will go, wherever you lodge I will lodge, your people shall be my people, and your God my God. Wherever you die I will die, and there be buried. May the LORD do so and so to me, and more besides, if aught but death separates me from you!" What kind of woman was Naomi, that she could inspire such loyalty in Ruth!

When the old widow and the young widow reached Bethlehem, crops were good again. But Naomi's fields had long gone unplanted, and the two women had to scrape for a living. They did manage to live; and this was largely due to Ruth's resourceful work in the grain fields around Bethlehem. Chapters 2 and 3 of the book of Ruth tell how Naomi, still much concerned about Ruth's future, helped her daughter-in-law to win a good man for a husband.

When Ruth's first child was born, Naomi was overjoyed. She was not exactly a grandmother; but Ruth was so dear to her that she loved Ruth's baby boy as her own child. Chapter 4 tells about her hour of glory. The women, who a little earlier had noticed how changed and sad she was, now share her joy. "Blessed is the LORD who has not failed to provide you today with an heir! May he become famous in Israel! He will be your comfort and the support of your old age, for his mother is the daughter-in-law who loves you. She is worth more to you than seven sons!" Naomi took the little boy into her arms and loved him as if he were her own son. They called him Obed.

Naomi's joyful pride over Ruth's son would have been even bigger had she known that the little one there in her arms was to be the grandfather of Israel's second and most famous king, David. And her wonderment would have been endless had she been able to see across twelve centuries to the birth of another child at Bethlehem, a descendant of the child she was holding, Jesus son of Mary.

Words cannot do justice to Naomi. Maybe no one should try to describe a woman like her; the book of Ruth has already done the perfect job. It is enough simply to admire and love her, and to thank God for having made such a woman and for letting us know about her. Widows in particular should recognize in Naomi's closeness to God the only path that will lead them out of their grief back to joy. They should see that God himself can be their mainstay, as he was Naomi's, and that his love can heal the wound left in their lives by the death of a husband.

Reading the book of Ruth will also make us more aware of the many women of today whose loving concern for other people makes them very much like Naomi. Their love for us is a revelation of God's; his concern for us is expressed in theirs. Such women, like Naomi, rank high among the blessings God has given to the world. For them, God be praised and thanked.

Chapter 16

Harvest Love

BOAZ and RUTH   (Ruth)

THE strange world of the Bible may often puzzle us. But
this should come as no surprise. Since the Bible is most-
ly a record of what God did in the life of the Hebrew people
4000 to 2000 years ago, it would really be surprising if we
felt at home with the ways of those ancient Hebrews. Even
so, the careful reader will often feel the happy shock of
discovery when he finds that, under the unfamiliar surface
of things, the deeper realities of human life like birth, love,
marriage, and God, meant about the same to them as they
do to us.

The Old Testament's book of Ruth is a good place to
make this discovery. Its record of the wedding of Boaz
and Ruth is obscured for us by constant reference to a
marriage custom that is totally foreign to our ways. But
this obscurity does not keep us from recognizing in the love
that brought Boaz and Ruth together as man and wife the
same mysterious power that does the same thing today.

Ruth, the young widow who had accompanied her mother-
in-law, Naomi, back to Bethlehem, had to scrape for a
living by following the harvesters in Bethlehem's grain
fields to pick up unwanted bundles of barley. She was hard
at this humble work in a field that belonged to a relative

of her deceased husband when this man, whose name was Boaz, began to show a keen interest in her. His interest grew into loving admiration and tender concern. And his efforts to please her and win her attention became almost boyish. He had his workers drop good barley bundles on purpose for her to pick up. At the workers' meal he heaped more food into her plate than she could possibly eat. At the end of the day he invited her to come back the next morning.

When Ruth reported all this to Naomi, this resourceful woman, who was very much concerned about Ruth's future, decided to try her hand at match-making; and a skillful hand she had. It was clear to her that Boaz and Ruth were close to falling in love. But there was something else besides love that Naomi was counting on. Boaz was related by blood to Naomi's deceased husband, Elimelek, and so also to Ruth's deceased husband, Elimelek's and Naomi's son, Mahelon, who had died in Moab before Naomi and Ruth came to Bethlehem. According to ancient Hebrew custom, when a man died without children it was the duty of a close relative of the deceased to marry the widow and to have children by her who would continue the family name and inherit the family holdings. Naomi had no living sons, and so Ruth could not find a husband in Naomi's immediate family. But Boaz was a possibility; and Naomi decided to play on his sense of duty to determine him to take Ruth as his bride. Her plan was all the more likely to succeed because of the fact that Boaz and Ruth were more than a little interested in each other already.

Following her mother-in-law's instructions, Ruth went late one night to the threshing floor where a contented Boaz was sleeping after the day's work and a good meal. Ruth uncovered his feet and lay herself down near him. About midnight Boaz woke up and was startled to find a woman lying there at his feet. His astonishment turned into restrained joy when he found out who she was. Wasting no time, Ruth then and there asked Boaz to marry her. Boaz made no effort to hide his pleasure over Ruth's proposal and told her that he would be more than glad to have her if one doubt could be cleared up. Another man, who was more closely related to Ruth's deceased husband, had a prior right to Ruth if he wanted her. But if this man would waive his claim—and Boaz saw to it that he did—then she would certainly be the bride of Boaz. He told her to sleep on there at his feet until morning; which she did, and then returned to Naomi with a generous gift from Boaz and a full report of the night.

This incident has raised some eyebrows. But let us here accept it without burdening ourselves with the role of judge. Ruth did nothing that night that was clearly wrong; she did throw herself at Boaz in circumstances calculated to dispose him all the more to want her as his bride. But if we are prompted to say that Ruth at least acted imprudently, we must also honestly admit that we are in a poor position to pass judgment on her prudence since it depended on many factors unknown to us, such as Boaz' and Ruth's self-control.

Naomi's plan had worked perfectly. She could now leave it to Boaz. And chapter 4 tells us how well he handled the rest of Naomi's plan until the woman he loved became his bride, to have and to hold. God blessed them with a son, Obed, whose fame cannot be measured by human standards; he was privileged to be one of the great-grandfathers, twelve centuries removed, of Jesus.

The joy of that wedding of Boaz, who was no longer a young man, and Ruth the widow, can still be felt by reading the book of Ruth. This book, whose four chapters make it one of the shortest books of the Old Testament, is one of the most important documents ever written on family life. The men and women whose lives it records were deeply concerned about family unity and well practiced in family love. Ruth's loving affection for her mother-in-law makes her a sign to all times of the loving affection that should hold the members of a family close to one another even when distance must separate them. Boaz too was aware of his closeness to Naomi's family, a closeness all the more precious to him because of Ruth.

The warm love of parents for their children and of children for their parents, the love of brothers and sisters for each other, family love, can be the source of some of the deepest happiness available to man. Those who have experienced it will count it as one of God's best blessings on their lives. And true family love that looks to the happiness of those who are loved will not be a narrowing force, shutting people up within the limits of their immediate family. Rather, the give and take of love within one family will teach its members how to enter the lives of other people with some of the same warm spontaneity to which they have grown accustomed at home. And they will become a blessing of God on all who know them.

Chapter 17

Longing for a Child

ELKANAH and ANNA   (I Samuel 1-2)

A N old Hebrew priest named Eli was in charge of a shrine at Shiloh in southern Palestine. One day he saw there a woman whose odd movements made him think she was drunk. When he told her rather gruffly to go and get herself sobered up, she protested that she had not been drinking a thing. Then she gave him her story. Although the time and place are remote from us, this woman's story will find an echo in any reader's heart; it is the story of a woman's desire to bear a child.

Anna was her name. According to an awkward custom of her people she had to share her husband Elkanah, with another woman whose name was Peninnah. This other wife had given Elkanah sons and daughters; but Anna had not been able to bear him a single child. Elkanah's fruitful mate often boasted about her fertility to unproductive Anna, and deep resentment embittered Anna's life. Elkanah, who seems to have been unaware of the injustice involved in his polygamy, told Anna to quit hankering after a child. His words to her hold more than a hint of arrogant male self-sufficiency. "Why are you weeping and not eating? Why is your heart aching? Don't I mean more to you than ten sons?"

Anna had no answer for her husband's question. Instead,

she went in desperation to the shrine at Shiloh to pour out her heart's pain to God. While she was praying there, Eli found her and thought she was drunk. But after he had listened to her story, the old priest, convinced that he was speaking in God's name, promised her that her prayer for a child would be answered. His words cheered her and she went home believing that his promise would become a reality. When within a year she was the jubilant mother of a baby boy, she poured out her heart's glee in a song of thanks and praise to God for having been so good to her. Nor did she forget to take a couple of proud side-glances at Peninnah, her husband's other wife, who had made life miserable for her before. Anna's boy, Samuel, was to be one of Israel's most famous prophets.

The author of the first two chapters of the first book of Samuel where these events are recorded did not try to cover up the harsh realities of Hebrew life twelve centuries before Christ. He wrote about Elkanah's polygamy and pride, Peninnah's boasting, Anna's resentment and impatience, without passing judgment on any of these things. What mattered most to him was the fact that God was quietly working out his plan in the lives of these people by preparing for himself the prophet Samuel. Still, much can be learned also from Samuel's parents, especially from his mother. Notice how keenly Anna realized that a child is not only a woman's gift to a man but also God's gift to both of them. Out of that deep realization of God's fertile love came her prayer for a child, a prayer so expressive of her pent-up longing that old Eli mistook it for drunkenness.

Anna's prayer sprang from the bottom of a long frustrated desire. It was her flesh and blood and bone that prayed, as well as her spirit. And she got what she wanted. Her prayer for a child has been repeated by many a woman after her, and many a woman's child has been accepted as just as gracious a miracle of God as Anna's little Samuel.

Anna is a good example of that vigorous appeal to God which characterizes so much of Hebrew prayer. Some people are surprised at the boldness of the Old Testament Hebrews when they talked to God. Take the beginning of psalm 13 as a sample. "How long, O LORD? Will you utterly forget me? How long will you hide your face from me? How long shall I harbor sorrow in my soul, grief in my heart day after day? How long will my enemy triumph over me? Look, answer me, O LORD, my God!" Relentlessly the palmist drums out the words, "How long . . . how long . . . how long?" His impatience with God makes him demand, rather than politely request, God's help. If this is boldness, then God must be pleased with boldness in prayer, because the Old Testament psalms are God's own word expressing God's own idea about how we ought to treat him. If the psalms complain, then God must want to hear our complaints. If the psalms are daring and demanding, then God must be waiting for our daring demands.

There are times when trouble of one kind or another pushes our backs to the wall, times when there seems to be nobody who can help us. Anna felt that way about her inability to bear a child. The Christian wife today, too, may wish for children; or she might face sickness in the family, the tragedy of death, money worries, her husband's job insecurity, trouble with the children. When such problems bring on a feeling of helpless desperation the Christian woman must, like Anna, know how to pour out her heart's pain to God. And then, with his help, she must face her problems again and do what she can to solve them, calmly. If need be, she will renew this prayer and this effort every day. And God, in his own good time and not hers, will provide an answer.

PART THREE

In the Days of the Kings

Chapter 18

Despair or Joy

SAUL and AHINOAM (I Samuel 14)

WHEN a reluctant old Hebrew prophet poured scented oil over the head of a tall handsome Benjaminite named Saul, Israel had its first king. King Saul's wife, Ahinoam, bore him three sons and two daughters. Jonathan, first of their sons, was linked by unbreakable friendship to a young soldier named David who at first enjoyed the king's favor but later felt the sting of his hatred. Saul's younger daughter became David's first bride. Because of Saul's repeated failures to measure up to his duties as king, the old prophet Samuel who had anointed him king served him stern notice that no son of his would be his successor. Instead of a son it was his hated son-in-law, David, who took Saul's place as Israel's king.

The Hebrew writer of the Old Testament's book of

Samuel says no more about Ahinoam, Saul's wife and mother of his children. But nearly the whole book is taken up with the story of her puzzling husband.

King Saul began his reign with some promising military successes against Israel's southern enemy, the Philistines. But soon he took to disregarding the prophet Samuel's instructions. His pride was badly hurt by David's growing popularity and he tried to murder this young soldier who had served him bravely. Things went from bad to worse, with Israel's political fortunes often reflecting Saul's personal life, until on a battlefield in the hills of north-central Palestine the broken man threw himself onto his own sword and died.

Saul was forever fighting the Philistines and often he was the victor. But more dangerous enemies rose up inside him and he never saw them very clearly until his suicidal surrender. It was jealousy that almost drove him insane when dancing Israelite women sang, "Saul has struck down thousands, but David his ten thousands." His careless disregard of instructions received from God's spokesman, the prophet Samuel, got him in bad with God as well as with Samuel. Superstitious fear drove him to consult a professional witch even after he had banned all such women from his realm. Finally, his despairing conviction that God would never again look on him with favor pushed him to put an end to his shoddy life by his own hand.

King Saul's life has little if anything to offer us by way of positive inspiration in living. Still, the story of Saul ought to impress on us the fact that jealousy, disobedience to God, especially despair of God's mercy can all hurt a man and if left unremedied can make an irreversible tragedy out of life.

Christian husbands may often have to struggle against these same inside enemies that destroyed Saul. Jealousy

aroused by someone else's success can still make a man hard
and bitter when he should be praising God for his neighbor's
good fortune. Habitual disregard of God's known will can
make a man lose his awareness of God in his life. And this
loss of a sense of God's presence can lead to a skeptical
attitude about God in general and especially about God's
care for human life. Then when personal troubles strike
deep into a man, loss of a job, serious sickness or bitter
quarreling in the family, or serious sin, a man sometimes
looks around for a way out of it all, a way to shrug off from
his now unwilling shoulders the burden of responsibility
which he had taken on. Few such people take their own
lives as King Saul did; but many share something of his
despairing conviction that God no longer cares.

No easy answer to this problem like "leave everything to
God" will do, since the problem arises precisely because
most of the time God seems to leave everything up to you.
The answer is to be found not only in Jesus' sermon on the
mount where he said that we ought to be as untroubled
about our needs as the birds and the flowers about theirs,
but also in the garden of Gethsemani where he struggled
to submit his will to his Father's. "My God, my God, why
have you abandoned me!" was his cry on the cross before
it was ever yours. The fact that Jesus' abandonment by his
Father was followed by his resurrection from the dead gives
you the light you need on your own abandonment by God.
It too will end in joy if you keep on hoping in God your
Father and trusting that he will do for you what he did for
His Son.

Memory of the cross of Jesus must be our best remedy
against despair. The God whom we worship cared enough
about us to become man and share our human misery as well
as our joy so that we could share his glorious resurrection as
well as his cross. No wonder Saint Paul urged his Christians

to rejoice in the Lord always. Holy Mass is the living memorial of Jesus' death on the cross; but it is a living joyful Jesus whom we offer to God the Father and whom we receive in Holy Communion. Awareness of the fact that he belongs to us and we to him ought not only to keep us from falling into Saul's despair but should also fill our hearts, even in a whirl of trouble, with joy.

Chapter 19

A Son's Vocation

JESSE and WIFE   (I Samuel 16)

JESSE, whose grandmother Ruth had come to Bethlehem with Naomi, was living there with his family when one day the prophet Samuel paid him a visit. The Prophet's business was to find a successor to King Saul, who was ruling Israel badly and he knew that God wanted him to select Israel's new ruler from Jesse's sons.

When Samuel saw Eliab, he thought he had found his man in this tall young son of Jesse. But he learned from God that he was mistaken; so he asked for a look at the others. Abinadab, Shammah and four other young men were introduced to Samuel by their father. But when the prophet had looked them over, not a one of them satisfied him. So he asked Jesse, "Are these all the young men?" When Jesse told him that he had one more boy, his youngest, who was at the moment out tending the family's flocks, Samuel asked to see the young shepherd. The 16th chapter of the Old Testament's first book of Samuel, where this event is recorded, speaks well of the boy. "He was ruddy, and had beautiful eyes and attractive appearance." Samuel looked at him and decided at once that this shepherd boy was to be Israel's next king. There in the presence of all the family, Samuel poured precious oil on the young head of David and by that rite declared him king.

Some time passed before this youngster became king in fact. Meanwhile he saw a lot of trouble, first as King Saul's musician, then as his soldier, finally as an outlaw hated and hunted by the King he had served so well. In his dangerous outlaw days David provided for the safety of his father and mother by taking them to Moab, first homeland of his great-grandmother Ruth, where he left them in the keep of a friendly Moabite king. This is the last we hear about the parents of Israel's second and most famous king.

Jesse and his wife must have been mystified when the prophet Samuel anointed their youngest son as Israel's king. It seems that Jesse himself did not even consider David as a possible choice, since it was only as an afterthought that he introduced the boy to Samuel. However, once the parents realized that the prophet's choice was also God's they accepted it without question. In their acceptance of God's will for their son, strange as that divine choice must have seemed to them, Jesse and his wife are a sign to all parents that God has rights over their children which must be respected.

It may be that no prophet Samuel will come to parents today to tell them what God wants their sons and daughters to do and to be. But God has other ways of showing his choice. He shows it in the very decisions reached by the sons and daughters themselves, decisions that grow out of their own talents and inclinations. And since God wills that men and women should follow a way of life in keeping with their God-given natures, such decisions are signs of God's will and of a divine vocation.

Parents are in a delicate position here. The very fact that they are parents, sources of life to their children, makes them intensely interested in the ways of life opening out to their youngsters. Whether it is a question of a religious vocation in preference to marriage, or of a particular mate in marriage, or of one career rather than another, most parents are rightly concerned. In some parents this concern goes too far; and they try to control what they have no business trying to control, namely the free choice of God as made known in the responsible decisions of their sons and daughters. It is pathetic to see a young man so tightly tied to his mother's apron or to his father's wallet that he finds himself unable to decide important things for himself. His father tells him he is too young to get married, although he is three or four years older than his father when he took a wife. Son is reminded in countless way of his dependence on his father for a living; but father would be doing him a far greater service if he encouraged him to be independent, as independent as he was when he was this boy's age. This inability of some parents to remember when they were young would be harmless if it did not at times stunt the responsible initiative of their children. Deep resentment of children against their parents sometimes starts and grows in such over-productive care. If children must respect their parents as givers of life, parents must also learn to respect their children as responsible human persons mysteriously filled with possibilities for good that God, in unpredictable ways, will help them turn into realities.

Jesse and his wife loved David. But their love was generous, and they let him go even though he was young, when they knew that God wanted him somewhere else. And David loved them and took care of them in their old age even though he had a world of other troubles to occupy him at the time. Today things are much the same.

Chapter 20

Love Neglected

DAVID and MICHAL   (I Samuel 18)

THE first of King David's many wives was Michal, young-est daughter of King Saul. Their wedding, which is recorded in the 18th chapter of the Old Testament's first book of Samuel, was celebrated under the cloud of King Saul's mounting hatred for David. The jealous king had, in fact, arranged this marriage precisely in order to destroy David. His plan was crude, and the Bible does not spare its reader's sensibilities in describing the affair.

The price which the king demanded from David for Michal—in those days the groom paid the bride's father a fee—was a hundred foreskins of the Philistines, who were Israel's enemy to the south. King Saul thought that David would be killed in his attempt to meet this demand. But David was not killed, and when he presented his fee, Michal became his bride.

Michal loved David, and soon proved her love by ex-posing her life to the fury of her father by helping David escape from assassins sent by the king. Sometime during his long outlaw days when David was unable to be with Michal, King Saul gave her to another man; and David himself, during the same period, married two other wives. But after King Saul's suicide, when David had become

Israel's king at Hebron and was fighting the army that had been Saul's, he got Michal back again much to the grief of the man to whom Saul had given her.

After seven years at Hebron David managed to make Jerusalem his royal city and he built his palace there. Soon after this he arranged to have the ark of the covenant, which was a precious wooden box containing a copy of the ten commandments, removed from a private home to his part of the city. The transfer of this sacred box, which was one of the signs of God's presence among his people, was made by a procession of jubilant Hebrews who were immensely pleased with their King David. The king himself entered into the common joy with all his heart and soul. As the 6th chapter of the second book of Samuel says, "David was also dancing with all his strength."

Michal, who was watching all this, did not share her husband's merriment; in fact, she took the dimmest view of his part in the celebration. "Then the ark of the LORD came into the city of David. And as Michal, daughter of Saul, was looking out of the window, she saw King David dancing and leaping before the LORD, and despised him in her heart." When the celebrating had come to an end Michal told her husband with bitter contempt that, in her opinion, he had made a silly fool of himself by dancing in the procession. David, whose sudden contempt for her matched hers for him, threw up to her the memory of her unfortunate father and from that moment on had nothing more to do with her. So the bride who, as the Bible says, loved David, is now given her sad epitaph. "Michal, daughter of Saul, had no child to the day of her death."

Many factors led to the failure of this marriage: forced separation, David's polygamy, Michal's more or less willing acceptance of another man, their shared memory of the conflict between Michal's father and David, and finally the procession incident. But it seems that the main trouble between David and Michal was their lack of geniune respect for one another. On her side this disrespect came out into the open when she spoke her mind to David after she saw him dancing in the procession. On his side it was expressed by his contemptuous refusal to have anything more to do with her after feeling the cut of her tongue.

Christian husbands and wives can learn from the marriage of David and Michal the necessity of developing sincere respect for one another in all the details of their married life. This respect will grow and strengthen their mutual love only if they are aware of their immense worth as human persons. Every human person is God's masterpiece. All God's creatures are good and pleasing to him because he made them; but among His material creatures the human person is the best because the human person is the most God-like, able to think and love and to share thought and love with others. St. Paul says that man is God's glory, the sign of God's presence in his universe.

Many of us may keep this precious native worth of ours hidden under an unlovely crust of oddities, annoying ways, and even habits of sin. Still, a human person is God's masterpiece in spite of physical disfigurement or intellectual lack or moral disorder. This natural worth which even the shabbiest of us can never shake off is an inescapable reason why each husband and his wife should develop the habit of loving respect for one another. But there is a still more compelling reason that motivates those who have entered marriage as a sacrament made by Jesus Christ. In their life the husband somehow represents Christ and his wife represents the Church. St. Paul wrote in the 5th chapter of his letter to the Ephesians, "Let wives be subject to their husbands as to the Lord, because a husband is the head of his wife as also Christ is the head of the Church and Savior of his body. But as the Church is subject to Christ so also let the wives be subject to their husbands in everything. Husbands, love your wives as Christ also loved the Church and delivered himself up for her." So the Christian wife must learn to love and respect her husband not only because he is God's masterpiece but also because he represents Christ to her. And the Christian husband's loving respect for his wife must grow out of his keen realization that the privilege of representing Christ also obliges him to love his wife as Christ loves her.

It is a wonderful thing to see older married people whose love for one another has grown stronger and stronger with the long years of their thorough experience of one another; each by accepting the other had to take the bad as well as the good in the other. Their love grew strong not because he never in his life seemed foolish to her or because she never in her life spoke a sharp word to him, but because each of them saw through the odd habits and harsh words of the other with a sincere respect for the loved person.

Chapter 21

Unloving Husband

NABAL and ABIGAIL   (I Samuel 25)

SHEEP shearing was a time to celebrate in Israel. So when Nabal, a prosperous small-cattle farmer in southern Palestine, was shearing his sheep there he had a festive banquet prepared for his workers and friends.

King David, whose authority was still shaky because his predecessor Saul was still living and hunting him down, had been in Nabal's neighborhood for a while. David's men had been protecting Nabal's shepherds from rustlers and had not done any rustling themselves. So when David sent word to Nabal asking him for food supplies for his men, this was a polite way of reminding him to pay his debt.

But Nabal didn't see it that way. He met David's request with a contemptuous no, and then insulted the young king by referring to him as a runaway slave. When David was informed of Nabal's attitude, his own reaction was quick. He put on his sword and alerted his men for a fight with Nabal's household, swearing by his life to kill every male among them.

While on his way to make his oath good, David was met in a mountain pass by Abigail, Nabal's wife, who without her husband's knowledge had prepared the food supplies for which David had asked, and she gave them to him then and there. David was satisfied with the supplies, and much pleased by the woman who had brought them. He sent her home with his promise not to harm her husband.

Abigail found her husband at home, but he was too drunk with the wine of the sheep shearers' banquet to listen to her that night. When next morning she was able to tell him what she had done and how narrowly he had escaped David's sword, he suffered some kind of stroke. Another stroke ten days later killed him. As soon as David heard of Nabal's death he thanked God for the way the whole thing had turned out. Then he sent word to Abigail asking her to be his wife; and she came.

The sacred writer, recording this event in the 25th chapter of the Old Testament's first book of Samuel, places the blame for trouble in the Nabal-Abigail family squarely on the man of the house. Nabal is described as rough and uncouth; Abigail was a woman of good sense, and beautiful. He was ungrateful and contemptuous to David; she showed deep reverence for David's person, and offered to take on herself the blame for her husband's crude ways. Nabal's own servants said that he was a base rascal who would not listen to reason; these same servants approached Abigail with confidence, hoping that she would be able to save them from David's oath against their master.

How long Abigail had to put up with such a man, we are not told. She herself remarked to David that her husband was a worthless fool; so she must have had about all of him that she could take. No wonder that, as soon as Nabal had died shortly after his last drinking bout, Abigail had an eager yes for David's offer to take her as his wife. Whether she was happier in David's harem than she had been with Nabal is another thing we do not know.

When Christian husbands and wives read this chapter of the Bible they will see at once that Nabal and Abigail were no ordinary couple; Abigail was wonderfully good and Nabal was uncommonly bad. But the reader will also be able to see that Nabal's unusual badness was nothing but the advanced ugly growth of a selfish preoccupation with his own person and property and pleasure to the point of contempt for other people.

The person who felt Nabal's contempt more than anyone else was his wife. He did not love her; this is clear from the fact that he was not concerned about her happiness. He was too wrapped up in himself to see her as a person to be loved. Love for her would have urged him to change his crude ways and to do the things that would please her and make her want him for a husband. But he did not love her; instead, he treated her as he treated other people, with contempt; and she resignedly talked of him as a worthless fool.

The Christian husband must see his wife not only as the person in whom he hopes to find his happiness but even more as the person whose life he may fill with joy. And it doesn't take a lifetime of experience in loving and being loved to discover that the lover's own joy depends on the joy of the person he loves. Over the years he will not neglect even the little things that he knows will please her, such as the signs of attention and affection that meant so much to both of them earlier. And God, who united them to begin with, will see to it that they never drift apart.

Chapter 22

Absent Husband

URIAH and BATHSHEBA   (II Samuel 11-12)

URIAH, one of King David's loyal soldiers, was summoned by his king from a battle in Transjordan and given leave to visit with his beautiful wife, Bathsheba, at their home in Jerusalem. But Uriah, knowing that his fellow soldiers enjoyed no such privilege, would not take advantage of the king's favor; instead, he spent the night with his men.

The soldier must have been puzzled next day when King David insisted on having him as guest at a banquet for no apparent reason. After the banquet, in the course of which Uriah had gotten himself drunk, he still did not go home to his wife, as David hoped he would do, but again spent the night with the soldiers at Jerusalem.

Next morning David sent Uriah back to Transjordan with a letter to Joab who was field general of David's troops. A short time after delivering this letter Uriah was killed in battle at the city of Rabbah. Uriah never knew that his death had been planned, that the letter which he had handed to Joab contained instructions as to how its carrier was to be exposed to enemy swords, that his murderer was the ruler whom he had served loyally, King David.

From the beginning of the 11th chapter of the Old Testament's second book of Samuel, where this event is recorded, the sacred writer tells us the motive behind this murder. It was Bathsheba, Uriah's only wife, whom David wanted for his harem even if he had to kill her husband to get her. David had seen her bathing, had learned whose wife she was; and she had accepted an invitation to come to his palace. When a little later she informed him that she had his child in her womb, King David sent for her husband and gave him leave to spend some time at home with her. David hoped that Bathsheba's child would then be thought to be Uriah's.

But after failing twice in his efforts to get Uriah and Bathsheba together, David changed his plan. Another way of handling the problem would not only relieve him of any trouble with Uriah but would also give him Bathsheba for keeps; Uriah had to be killed. But the thing had to be done carefully. It must not look like murder. The king's good name must not be jeopardized. Only Joab would know that his soldier's death at Rabbah was not an accident of war. After Uriah's killing, David had the hypocrisy to tell Joab, "Let not this affair pain you, for the sword eats up one as well as another."

Bathsheba mourned her husband's death, then went to David to be his wife. Their baby son died soon after birth; and the king learned from the prophet Nathan that the death of this child was God's way of punishing David's double crime against Uriah. David expressed geniune sorrow for what he had done, and Nathan assured him of God's ready forgiveness. Then David comforted Bathsheba over the loss of her child and brought her into his harem. The second son she bore him was Solomon, Israel's magnificent third king and Jesus Christ's great-grandfather ten centuries removed.

Trouble came into the Uriah-Bathsheba home when he was away at war. The long forced separation of this soldier husband from his wife, although it does not excuse her weak submission to the lustful wishes of her king, did create an unhealthy marriage situation. As far as we can tell from the biblical record, Uriah was perfectly faithful to his wife; it was David, and Bathsheba, who were responsible for the trouble. Bathsheba was the one who weakened under the strain of forced separation from her husband; the grip of their love was not strong enough to hold her to him when he was away from home.

Christian husbands and wives also must face the possibility of forced separation at times. Armed service, the demands of a job, sickness—any of these things can deprive them of each other's presence. Then, while the ordinary physical expression of their love is impossible, their love itself must be strong enough to unite their minds and hearts even across many miles and long months. They must learn, even before the unwanted separation comes, that the physical expression of their love is not the only tie binding them to one another. Christ himself, mysteriously and really present in each of them, is the strongest bond uniting them.

If they keep themselves aware of the fact that their sexual union is itself their constant part in making Christ's sacrament of marriage a reality, they will find Him uniting their minds and hearts even when they are miles and months apart.

Chapter 23

Man with a
Thousand Women

SOLOMON and WIFE   (I Kings 3)

Ancient Israel reached its political peak during the reign of Solomon ten centuries before Christ. For so small a kingdom Solomon was a very pretentious king. Everything he did was done on a sweeping scale.

The Old Testament's first book of Kings (sometimes referred to as the third book of Kings) tells of his ruthless destruction of political enemies, among whom his own half-brother Adoniah and David's old field general Joab were struck down. Solomon's burnt-offerings, animals sacrificed to God, numbered many thousands. His food was sumptuous even for a king. He had 40,000 horses and 1400 chariots at his service. His reputation as a wise man was world wide. He could talk on any subject, from cedar trees and hyssop plants to birds and snakes. He built a magnificent temple to God in Jerusalem which lived on as a vivid Hebrew memory even after it was destroyed by the Babylonians in the 6th century B.C. And for himself he made an equally magnificent palace. His building projects were vast and costly. He had a fleet of ships plying the Red Sea. Everything he used, from his royal throne to his drinking cups, had to be of the best material. All in all, Solomon was immensely pleased with himself and sure that he deserved the best and the most of everything.

King Solomon also married on a grand scale. Other Hebrews before him, including his father David, had taken more than one wife. But Solomon seems to have outdone them all. His marriage to an unnamed Egyptian princess, which is recorded in chapter 3, was only the first of a long string of royal weddings. Even allowing for some exaggeration in biblical numbers, the sum total of his women must have been staggering. The Bible says, "He had seven hundred wives, princesses, and three hundred concubines."

For the most part the Bible records the lives of polygamists like Abraham, Jacob, and David without saying that there was anything wrong with their polygamy. But after telling about the thousand women who stood at Solomon's pleasure, the Bible adds a stern judgment. "And his wives turned his heart." Solomon violated the first commandment by worshiping the gods of his wives and so betrayed Israel's hard-won faith in one God. He worshiped Ashtart, the Phoenician fertility goddess, an Ammonite god named Milcom, and the Moabites' god Chemosh which his great-great-grandmother Ruth had laid aside in order to surrender herself forever to Naomi's true God.

For all these outrages to God's honor Solomon was punished, not only in his own person but also in his successors; and the Bible gives no indication that he ever had a change of heart before his death. Where was all his wisdom now? Gone, destroyed by the social custom of polygamy with its attendant evils.

Christian husbands and wives probably don't as a rule think or say much about polygamy. For most of them it is not a real problem. But in parts of Africa polygamy is today one of the main obstacles to the acceptance of Christian teaching. And it required an act of Congress to outlaw in the United States the polygamous practice of the Mormons. These facts, as well as the marriage customs of the Old Testament Hebrews, prove that the blessings of monogamy are not to be taken for granted.

It is true that some of the Old Testament Hebrews were convinced that marriage ought to be the union of one man with one woman for life. This is the main point of the Old Testament's Song of Songs, where the shepherd says of his bride, "One alone is my dove, my perfect one." But it was Jesus Christ and His Church whose doctrine about marriage has done most to eliminate polygamy.

The attempt of one man to be the husband of more than one woman at a time is an insult to the dignity of woman. Is she or is she not a human person basically equal to the male in intelligence and in her power to love? The polygamist, even if he is unaware of the fact, says in practice that a woman is not basically his equal. The polygamist cannot grasp the principle behind St. Paul's claim in the 7th chapter of his first letter to the Corinthians that the husband's debt to his wife is equal to her debt to him. Christian women will want to give credit and a deeply loving thanks where credit and thanks are due—to Christ who understands better than anybody else the true worth of his creature woman and who loves each woman more dearly than any husband can.

Christian husbands will also give credit to Christ for remaking monogamous marriage; no thinking man would feel capable of doing justice to more than one wife. Solomon, for all his wisdom, was not wise enough to see this. But someone greater than Solomon has taught us the truth.

Chapter 24

God Speaks Through Men

NAAMAN and WIFE   (II Kings 5)

Playing in the water of the Jordan River gives you a bit of relief from the heavy heat of earth's deepest valley. But for centuries people have been swimming in that muddy creek also because Jesus Christ stood in it one day to be baptized by his cousin John.

Even before its waters ever washed the body of Christ the Jordan had long been regarded by the Jews as a sacred stream since it was the miraculous source of life to the long fertile valley which ran through the length of the land that God had given them. The fifth chapter of the Old Testament's second book of Kings (sometimes referred to as the fourth book of Kings) records another kind of miracle which God worked in the Jordan's water.

In the ninth century B.C., bands of Syrian raiders used to strike across Israel's northern border for their loot. One such raid netted among other things an Israelite girl who became the slave of the wife of Naaman, who was the commander of the Syrian army. The girl liked her mistress and took a geniune interest in her family. When she learned that Naaman himself was a leper she felt pity for him and decided to speak to his wife about a possible cure. Remembering the Hebrew prophet Elisha who was living in central Palestine, the girl told Naaman's wife, "If only my master were in the presence of the prophet who is at Samaria! He would heal him of his leprosy."

The girl's suggestion was taken up, and soon Naaman was on his way to see the prophet. But the Syrian leper was surprised and his pride was hurt when Elisha did not come out to meet him personally but simply sent a messenger instead. And when the messenger told him to go and wash in the Jordan River seven times, Naaman thought he was being treated as a fool and stubbornly affirmed that the Amana and the Pharpar, rivers of Syria, were better than the Jordan to wash in. But as he was going off in a huff, his own slaves talked with him until they convinced him that he ought to do what the prophet had said. "He went down and dipped in the Jordan seven times according to the word of the man of God, and his flesh was once again like the flesh of a little child, and he was clean."

Naaman, the former leper, went back to thank the prophet and to profess his faith in the true God of Israel who had cured him. When he also tried to make a gift to Elisha, the prophet refused to accept it. Then he asked and received permission to take back to his homeland some of the soil of Israel to help him remember the land where he had found God's blessing. He also asked God to pardon him if he seemed to take part in the worship of the false gods back in Syria, gods in which he no longer believed. Then Elisha wished him the Hebrew goodby, "Go in peace." His wife and the Israelite slave girl must have been happy to have him back again cured of his disease and a believer in the true God who had worked his cure.

Naaman's easily offended pride almost made him a leper for life. But somehow, even though it cost him a struggle, he managed at crucial moments to listen to the sound advice of other people. His wife, her slave girl, the Hebrew prophet and his messenger, Naaman's own slaves—all these people loved him and wanted to help him. Finally, after his seven dips in the Jordan River on that wonderful day when his leprous skin turned smooth and clean like the skin of a child, he could see that God's love for him had been quietly at work in their's.

He must have seen too that he had been cured of an illness worse than leprosy. He told Elisha, "Your servant will henceforth offer neither burnt-offering nor sacrifice to other gods, but to the LORD." Saved now from the unhappiness and frustration that were bound to result from his former polytheistic worship, he began to experience the joy of believing in the one true God, the Creator and Healer of man. His mind as well as his skin had been made new.

The habit of seeing God's love at work in the people with whom we live is an important part of Christian wisdom. Happy is the man who has learned to see in his wife not only a much loved and needed person but also a sign and instrument of the mighty love of God who gave her to him in the first place. And the wife who can see in her husband not only the man who loves and works hard to make life good for her and for their family but also the man through whom God himself loves her and takes care of her—she is a wise woman indeed. For children of such parents God's love will be an ever present reality in the very love that goes out to them from their parents.

God, as the prophet Isaiah said, is a hidden God. Like Naaman, we may have to swallow our pride and become like children in order to find him in the people we think we know so well.

Chapter 25

A Child Is God's Gift

FRIENDS of ELISHA (II Kings 4)

NINE centuries before Christ, the prophet Elisha used to travel back and forth between Mount Carmel and Shunem in north central Palestine. At Shunem he often enjoyed a meal which a generous woman there gladly prepared for him. She and her aging husband decided to furnish a special room in their house where the prophet could stay when he was teaching in their town.

Elisha was grateful for these favors, and one spring day he asked his friend if there was anything he could do for her. When he was reminded by his servant of the fact that this woman had no child, the prophet told her that within a year she would be holding her own baby boy in her arms. Thinking of her husband's age, she told Elisha that he must be joking and begged him not to give her any false hopes. But he said no more, and left town. Next spring she gave birth to a boy.

When the youngster was old enough to do a little work in the fields, he went out one morning with the harvesters to help his father. A hot sun lay heavy on the field, and during the morning the boy came to his father and complained of a severe headache. So his father had him taken home to his mother. She held him in her lap, desperately trying to keep him alive; at noon she saw her God-sent child was dead in her arms. She took him up to Elisha's room and laid him on the prophet's bed. Then, although her husband was a bit reluctant to let her go, she saddled an ass and rode off for Mount Carmel to see Elisha. She told her servant, "Hurry! Don't stop me on this ride unless I tell you to."

When the prophet saw her coming, he sent his servant to ask her if everything was going well with her family. She said yes, and then kept on riding up the mountain until she had come to Elisha. There she stopped, ran up to the prophet, and threw her arms around his legs. The prophet's servant was about to shove her away, but Elisha stopped him. "Let her be. She has had a bitter experience, and the LORD has hidden it from me and has not told me." When she told him that her child was lying lifeless on the prophet's bed back in Shunem, he sent his servant to touch his own walking stick to the boy's face. But the mother let him know that she would be satisfied with nothing but the presence of the prophet himself in her stricken home. So to her home he went.

On their way to Shunem, they met Elisha's servant, who told him that nothing had happened when the walking stick had touched the boy's face. "The child did not wake up." When they came into the town, Elisha went into the room alone and closed the door. After praying to God, he went to the bed and stretched the full length of his body on the body of the boy, hands to hands and eyes to eyes and mouth to mouth. After a while the boy's body grew warm, and Elisha got up and walked around a bit. Then he repeated his previous action, and the boy sneezed seven times and opened his eyes. He called the boy's mother and gave him to her alive. Again she fell at his feet, speechless this time with joy over what had happened.

This friend of Elisha was neither the first nor the last woman whose heart has been shattered by the loss of a child. But she was one of the few mothers who have experienced the double joy of giving life to a child and of seeing life return to that same child. Most women who see their children die must accept the loss with no prophet to warm a little body back to life. The death of a child sometimes leaves the mother—and the father too—inconsolable, like the mothers of Bethlehem who would not be comforted because their baby boys had been killed by Herod. Such grief is perfectly understandable to anyone who knows that the miracle of human life links mother and child in a loving embrace that cannot be broken without pain. Whoever thinks such tears are unworthy of a Christian should recall the tears of Christ at the tomb of his friend Lazarus. But the real problem is not the stopping of tears; they cannot and need not be stopped. The real problem is understanding how a child's death can fit into God's loving providence. The death of a child, filled to exploding with all the promise of life—this, as far as ordinary human values can tell us, must seem utterly meaningless. We need the help of something more than ordinary human values here.

Light on this problem comes to us from the crucifix. Every Christian believes that the death of Christ is somehow the cause of our salvation from sin, somehow the force that moves us towards eternal union with God. This seems absurd, that God should use such a means—the death of his Son—to accomplish his purpose. Human reason rightly says that God could have accomplished his purpose in a less painful way. We simply do not know—because God has not told us—why he chose to act the way he did. But he requires this of us: to believe that his infinite wisdom, as well as human malice and jealousy and indifference, was at work in the death of his Son.

Every Christian mother who has been parted violently from her child must somehow learn to live by the light of this truth. Mary herself at the foot of the cross learned that God had a supremely wise purpose in allowing his Son, who was her Son also, to die the death of a criminal. By faith we know what that purpose was, and so we know that the death of Christ fits into God's loving providence. And if this is so, then there is no real problem about accepting the fact that the death of a child also fits into that same loving providence; tears there will be, and broken hearts, but no problem for the mind.

But there is even more reason for joy within the grief of the Christian mother who has lost her child. She, along with all other Christians, believes in the reality of the life of the world to come and so ought to be confident that her child enjoys that life with God. Still more. She believes, on the authority of Christ, in the resurrection of the body. The miracle which filled with wordless wonder the heart of the woman whose son was warmed to life by the prophet Elisha —this miracle Christ will work for the Christian mother too. Only she must wait a while.

Chapter 26

A Wife Forgiven

HOSEA and GOMER   (Hosea)

PEOPLE who think that the Bible is a collection of nice "Bible Stories" are in for a wholesome surprise when they pick their Bible up from its place of honor in the home and begin to read it. Its realism in recording and interpreting real human life is often jolting, as it was meant to be. Some of the sermons you will find in the Old Testament books of prophets would be considered by many people as too raw for modern ears. Many people are used to thinking of God and real human life as two unrelated things. They are not well attuned to the exciting biblical idea that God is inextricably involved in all human life, good and bad.

The Old Testament's book of Hosea (same as Osee) records the stubborn love of Hosea for his wife. Their marriage relation became in Hosea's mind a vivid sign of Israel's relation to God; and this was the main point of his book. Although the two relationships, Israel's to God and Hosea's to his wife, are often mixed up in the prophet's description of things, the facts of his married life are somewhat as follows.

Hosea, a Hebrew prophet (one whose job it was to speak in God's name to the Hebrew people), married Gomer, who, besides being the object of Hosea's deep love, was a harlot.

God's will was somehow in this marriage; either Hosea had received some kind of indication that God wanted him to marry Gomer, or else afterwards he could look back and see that God's will had somehow been accomplished in their troubled lives.

A boy, a girl, and then another boy were born to them. Sometime in the course of their married life, Gomer got tired of Hosea and began running after other men; soon she was selling herself to anybody who wanted her. Hosea knew what his wife was doing and, deeply hurt, threatened to punish her. But she left him and her family to go her own selfish way, apparently forgetting her husband completely.

But even if she could close her eyes to him, he could not get her out of his mind. He found that he loved her in spite of what she was doing to him; he needed her and wanted her back. Finally, Gomer herself saw what a fool she had been to throw away so fine a man as Hosea. She rediscovered her love for him and went back to him. Before taking her again Hosea tested her by making her live by herself for a time. He told her, "Many days you shall wait for me; you shall not play the harlot or belong to any man; I in turn will wait for you."

After she passed his test, Gomer was to be Hosea's wife again. Both of them looked forward with joy to this reunion. No mention is made of Hosea's sense of honor. Many a self-respecting male would probably have written such a wife off his book. But not Hosea. If he had a sense of honor it was overpowered by his indestructible love for Gomer. His love for her not only made him willing to take her back; it urged him to forgive her all that she had done to him. What God said to Israel, Hosea said to Gomer: "I will espouse you to me forever: I will espouse you in right and in justice, in love and in mercy; I will espouse you in fidelity, and you shall know the LORD."

The record of this marriage is bound to make Christian husbands and wives more aware of the need for a spirit of forgiveness in their homes. Although the offenses that need forgiving are seldom as serious as the sins of Gomer, no Christian family can survive unless its members are ready to forgive and forget.

Jesus Christ made forgiveness the main point of the *Our Father* when He said at its conclusion, "For if you forgive others when they offend you, your heavenly Father will forgive you too. But if you do not forgive others when they offend you, your heavenly Father will not forgive you for your offenses."

Jesus' readiness to forgive offenses won for Him the wonderful accusation that He was the friend of sinners. And when He was dying on the cross He prayed for the men who had put him there, "Father, forgive them because they do not know what they are doing."

It should not be so hard for us to forgive others once we are aware of our own need for the same from them and from God. Even Hosea's spirit of forgiveness, generous as it was, resulted partly from his own felt need for Gomer. So it must be in every marriage and in every family. Our need for being loved is one of our reasons for loving. Our spirit of forgiveness will often depend on our sense of need for being forgiven.

Chapter 27

God's Great Mercy

AHAB and JEZEBEL (I Kings 16-22)

THE original Hebrew kingdom, for which God had promised King David an unending line of successor sons,
split into two warring factions right after the death of
David's son Solomon. All through Solomon's reign this fatal
split was in the making. No people could long put up with
his abusive administration. After the split the rebel kings
lived at Samaria in central Palestine until their city, and their
kingdom, was destroyed by the Assyrians in 721 B.C., while
the Davidic kings maintained Jerusalem as their royal city
until it too was destroyed by the Chaldean conquerors of the
Assyrians in 587 B.C. And so, early in the sixth century B.C.
all trace of political power had disappeared from both lines
of Hebrew kings.

This period from the tenth to the sixth centuries B.C. was
the age of the Hebrew prophets, those spokesmen for God
who had to cry doom more often than joy on God's divided
people and their kings. The Old Testament's books of
Kings give us an outspoken record of the activities of these
kings. No royal crime is glossed over; and the occasional
praiseworthy actions of a Hebrew king are duly praised.

One of the most wayward of these kings was Ahab; and
one of the biggest reasons for his waywardness was one of

his wives, Jezebel. Their story is told from the 16th to 22nd chapters of the first book of Kings (sometimes referred to as the third book of Kings).

Jezebel was not an Israelite, but the daughter of the king of Sidon, a Phoenician city to the north of Palestine. One of the first things Ahab did on marrying her was to worship her Phoenician god and to build a temple for it in Samaria. When the Hebrew prophet Eliah worked some drastic wonders in his efforts to get Ahab to change his ways, Jezebel was down on the prophet with cold fury and he had to run from the country to escape her murderous intentions. But the prophet was soon to return and the king would soon wince under his accusing finger. This affair is recorded in chapter 21.

A man named Naboth owned a vineyard next to the king's property in Samaria. Ahab wanted to get this vineyard, but Naboth refused to sell it. The king sulked over this and wouldn't eat. When Jezebel learned the reason for his mood, she made light of the problem and told him how he could get the vineyard without any trouble. Her plan was simple; have two unscrupulous characters publicly accuse Naboth of cursing God and the king, and then the people would stone him. All this was done just as Jezebel planned, and Ahab went to take possession of the dead man's vineyard. He thought his way was clear.

But he was mistaken. The prophet Eliah was back in his hair. Eliah knew what had happened and who was responsible for Naboth's death. He met his king right there in the murdered man's vineyard and gave him the tongue-lashing of his life. It contained a statement of fact and a threat. The fact was that although Ahab did not seem concerned about this, his and Jezebel's crime had been done in the sight of God. The threat was that Ahab would be punished for his crime by the loss of all his male descendants and that Jezebel would be killed and then eaten by dogs. Both these threats were later made good by the violent Jehu whom the prophet Elisha commissioned for this grim job.

Eliah's threat made an impression on the guilty king. As the Bible says, "When Ahab heard these words, he tore his clothes and put sackcloth next to his flesh and fasted. And he would go to bed in sackcloth and walk about in silence." This is the best thing the Bible has to say about Ahab. His sincere repentance, short as it was, won for him some measure of God's mercy. God said to Eliah, "Have you seen Ahab humbling himself in my presence? Because he has done so, I will not bring on the evil in his days. But in the days of his son I will bring the evil on his house." Later Ahab fell back into his old ways; he died on a battle field after a vain attempt to have the enemy Syrians kill another man instead of him.

Anyone who reads the biblical record of Ahab and Jezebel will see the extremes of malice and hypocrisy to which neglect of God's will can lead a man and a woman. On the constructive side there is very little to look for in their life. But that little is important. At one point in his reckless life, sincerely ashamed of what he had done, Ahab humbled himself before God and won God's mercy. Christians too need to be keenly aware of God's mercy not only as a truth of their faith to be believed but as the love of God going out to a real individual like Ahab. No living person, no matter what he has done, can rightly say that things are hopeless for him, that he is outside the reach of God's love. Jesus Christ told his apostle Peter to forgive the same sinner, if necessary, seventy times seven times.

Chapter 28

Children and the Future

ISAIAH and WIFE   (Isaiah 7-8)

WHILE the little kingdom of Judah was struggling for survival in the eighth century before Christ, its capital city, Jersualem, was put under siege by the armies of Syria and Israel. Inside the city, King Ahaz, afraid of the threatening destruction, thought that his only hope was to ally himself with the giant Assyrian power centered in Nineveh. With Assyria on his side, he hoped to be relieved of pressure from the two smaller kingdoms.

The prophet Isaiah, who made it his business to talk to King Ahaz, admitted the danger presented by the armies of the Syria-Israel alliance. But he also saw that a heavy price would have to be paid for Assyrian protection—a price which would involve the acceptance of Assyria's gods into the Hebrew religion. So he tried to convince the king not to go begging to Assyria, but to hold out against the besieging armies and to put his trust in the true God to save the city and its people. Any other course of action, either an attack on the Syria-Israel armies or alliance with Assyria, would plunge the kingdom of Judah to its ruin.

Isaiah failed to make his point with King Ahaz, who decided to ask Assyria for help. The second book of Kings tells about his deal with Tiglath-Pileser, the Assyrian king.

"I am your slave and son. Come up and save me from the hand of the kings of Syria and Israel who are rising against me." This decision was the root of immense harm to the people of Judah, and ultimately led to the destruction of their city and to their long Babylonian captivity.

Our main interest here does not lie in the fact that Isaiah failed to teach King Ahaz to trust in God, but rather in the part played by Isaiah's family in his work as a prophet. Not much is said about his wife and children, but the little that we do know is worth close attention. He refers to his wife as the prophetess, and gives the names of two of his sons. They are odd names, and it is likely that the boys were not called by these names in everyday life. Shear-Jashub was one, and in Hebrew this means "a part will come back." The other was Maher-Shalal Hash-Baz, which means hurry-plunder-rush-rob.

To the first boy, whose name spoke of a part that would come back, the prophet pointed as a sign of God's promise to bring back a favored part of his people after their long exile. The boy with the longer name was born during the crisis of King Ahaz's decision. To this boy, whose name recalls the violence of battle, Isaiah pointed as a sign of God's promise to relieve the people of Jerusalem from the siege. Before this boy would be old enough to say "father" or "mother," the Syria-Israel armies would be beaten down and plundered by the mighty Assyria and so would no longer be a threat to the kingdom of Judah.

God's promises were signified by these two boys and their strange names. Isaiah and his wife looked to their children as signs of a hopeful future for the whole people of Judah. In this vision they were like all other fathers and mothers who have ever dreamed of the future opening out for their sons and daughters. They looked at their children not only as individuals who would have a life of their own, but also as the bearers of hope for the whole people.

The Hebrews of Isaiah's time held that the human spirit survived the body in some vague way; but they had no idea of a happy immortality in the next world. This world here was the place of happiness, and immortality belonged to the family here more than to the individual person later. If a man could live to see his grandchildren—and better still his great-grandchildren—he was assured of a lasting place in their memory. Something of his character, his habits, something of himself, would live on in them.

This is the mentality which explains the intense desire of the Old Testament Hebrews to have children and the deep disappointment of a husband or wife who were not blessed by God with a child. Jesus Christ has taught us to hope not only for a conscious survival in a world beyond space and time, but also for a personal happiness which will surpass every imaginable joy. And so the desire for family immortality here on earth is not generally as intense among Christians as it was among the Old Testament Hebrews. But who can deny that this desire is still very much alive in any old man who grows young again by looking into the faces of his grandchildren, hoping they will remember him when he is gone, hoping they will receive a good impression of him and that their memory of him will help to make them happy and the bearers of happiness to others?

Children are signs of hope today just as Isaiah's boys were signs of hope for Judah's future in the eighth century before Christ. And the joy of parents who see themselves not only increased and multiplied in their children, but also projected into their children's future—this joy is one of God's blessings to married people. The Church still prays psalm 128 which sings about the joy of a husband and father and wishes him this blessing, "May you see your children's children." The wisdom of the Old Testament's book of Proverbs is as up to date as ever. "Grandchildren are the crown of old men, and the glory of children is their parentage."

When children can look with pride at their fathers, then fathers can be happy and thank God for the fact that they will live on in the memory, in the habits, in the persons of their children.

PART FOUR
Exile and After

Chapter 29

A Wife Is Joy

EZEKIEL and WIFE (Ezekiel 24)

EARLY in the sixth century B.C. came ancient Israel's darkest hour. Its pride and joy, Jerusalem, lay in ruins; its people were on their way as prisoners of war to Mesopotamia (modern Iraq). One of these deported Jews was the prophet Ezekiel, whose thankless job it was to interpret for his people the calamitous events that had fallen on them and try to give them hope for a better future which only their children would ever see.

Interpreting the events meant making his people aware of the fact that their wretched condition was to be found in their own lives. For a long time they had been disobeying God's laws and had not been sorry about it; now God was punishing them.

Ezekiel gave out God's message by means of lively symbols, and sometimes he even acted out his symbols in person.

One of his favorite ideas was marriage. Marriage was something people could understand. So he used it to explain something they didn't understand very well, namely Israel's relation to God. How was Israel related to God? As a wife to her husband. How did God love Israel? As a husband loves his wife. How did God act when Israel worshipped other gods and disobeyed His laws? Like a husband when his wife is running after other men.

In chapter 16 of his book, Ezekiel compares the Israelite people to a female baby abandoned by its father and mother to die in an open field. God saw the pitiful child, saved its life and raised it until by His loving care it grew up to be a beautiful girl. God loved this girl, chose her for His bride, married her, and by His lavish attentions made her lovelier still. But for some unaccountable reason she tired of God and became a harlot. Then comes what may be the most biting piece of irony ever written. God tells his harlot wife that, although as a general rule such a woman receives pay from the men who use her, she has been shamelessly paying men to use her. God then tells her that he is going to be pitiless in punishing her until she realizes what an enormous evil she has done to herself and to him. Finally, God gives her undeserved hope by assuring her, "I will re-establish my covenant with you, that you may know that I am the LORD, that you may remember and be covered with confusion, and that you may be utterly silenced for shame when I pardon you for all you have done." The prophet who wrote this must have had a deep knowledge of the facts of married life and a keen feeling for the value of fidelity.

Ezekiel takes up this theme again in chapter 23. This time he writes about two sisters, Oholah representing the (northern Hebrew kingdom) and Oholibah (the southern kingdom). Both sisters were God's wives. Oholah, the older of the two, also became a harlot and brought herself to ruin. Oholibah, even though she saw what had happened to her sister, became worse. God then threatened and punished His unfaithful wives without holding out any hope for a future reconciliation.

If God himself had not inspired his prophet to write such things, probably no one would have dared to speak of God's harlot wives. The idea is revolting, as it was meant to be. Sin is revolting; and the prophet was talking about sin. He had to make his pople understand what they had done to themselves and to God.

Again in chapter 24 Ezekiel uses the marriage relationship as a symbol of his people's experience. But this time the prophet did not simply make up a story in order to make his point. The symobl was itself a reality; it was the death of his wife. Before she died God had told him it would happen. "Son of man, by a sudden blow I am taking away from you the delight of your eyes, but do not mourn or weep or shed any tears. Groan in silence." When his wife died, Ezekiel did as he had been told; he kept his grief locked up in his own heart.

The prophet was forbidden to show any signs of his heart's pain over the death of his wife. This was to be an indication to his people that it would do them no good to grieve over the death of their sons and daughters. All these things, the delight of their eyes and the pride of their hearts, were gone because of their sins; and grief would not change the disaster.

The fact that Ezekiel's wife was an apt symbol of all that was lovely and delightful to the Jews is a clear sign of what she meant to Ezekiel himself. She was the delight of his eyes and the pride and joy of his heart. The Christian wife too must never stop trying to be all of that to her husband. His hope that she would be was one of his reasons for marrying her.

Chapter 30

Faithful Wife

JOACHIM and SUSANNA (Daniel 13)

S HORTLY before the time of Christ the Jews of Alexandria in Egypt added to their Bible a tiny book called Susanna. Because a young man named Daniel is a key figure in the story which it tells, this book was joined to the book of the prophet Daniel in early Christian times and there you will find it today as chapter 13. It tells the story of the wife of Joachim, who was a wealthy and influential Jew in Babylon (in modern Iraq) in the sixth century B.C.

The parents of Susanna had brought her up well; both by instruction and example they had taught her to practice her Jewish religion with a loving faith in God. She was also a very beautiful woman.

The little book is all about one event in Susanna's life. The sacred writer hoped that we, his readers, would learn a lesson from that event.

Two elderly men, who were acting as judges for the Jewish people in Babylon, used to spend a lot of time at Joachim's house. Both of them became infatuated over Joachim's lovely wife, and when each discovered the other's desire for her they tried to threaten her into letting them use her as they wanted.

They hid in her garden until she was alone. Then they

surprised her and told her that if she would not agree to satisfy their lust they would accuse her of adultery and have her stoned to death.

She refused to give in to them and screamed for help. When help came, these two highly respected judges had their accusation ready. They told Susanna's slaves that they had caught her sinning with a young man who, they said, had been too strong for them to hold and so had escaped.

Next day, in the presence of her family and friends, Susanna was accused and condemned to be stoned to death for adultery. It seems that nobody thought to question the word of these trusted judges until, after Susanna had prayed to God for help, a young man named Daniel shouted out from the crowd, "I am not responsible for the shedding of this woman's blood."

When people asked him what he meant, he told them that it was wrong to condemn a woman to death on the word of these two men without any further examination of the facts.

Then by clever questioning, Daniel convicted the two judges of deliberately planning the death of an innocent Jewess. She had been condemned by the lies of the very men who had tried to seduce her into doing the very thing for which they were condemning her to death. What a mess!

When young Daniel had straightened things out so that everybody knew the truth, the only thing left was to execute the death sentence on the judges who had passed it on an innocent person. This was done; and Susanna, saved from the brink of a shameful death, was reunited with her husband and children. Her family, along with her parents and friends, were immensely glad for her.

At least three lessons can be learned from this story; they are pointed out by the sacred writer at the end. Human testimony should not be accepted too readily. God is just, and so will save the innocent person from the injustice of men. Susanna, and any woman who acts as she did, is to be praised for her unshakable fidelity to her husband.

Doing what the two judges wanted would have kept them from passing the death sentence on her. But God saw everything, and she loved her husband; and so she told them no and took the consequences, faithful to Joachim and to God.

In the Old Testament, God himself praised the faithful wife. In the 31st chapter of the book of Proverbs God says, "When one finds a worthy wife, her value is far beyond pearls. Her husband, entrusting his heart to her, has an unfailing prize. She brings him good, and not evil, all the days of her life."

The Christian husband who has found such a wife will also appreciate what the Old Testament's book of Sirach (same as Ecclesiasticus) says in chapter 26:

"Happy the husband of a good wife, twice-lengthened are his days; a worthy wife brings joy to her husband, peaceful and full is his life.

"A good wife is a generous gift bestowed upon him who fears the LORD; be he rich or poor, his heart is content, and a smile is ever on his face.

"A gracious wife delights her husband, her thoughtfulness puts flesh on his bones; a gift from the LORD is her governed speech, and her firm virtue is of surpassing worth.

"Choicest of blessings is a modest wife, priceless her chaste person. Like the sun rising in the LORD's heavens, the beauty of a virtuous wife is the radiance of her home. Like the light which shines above the holy lampstand, are her beauty of face and graceful figure. Golden columns on silver bases are her shapely limbs and steady feet."

A faithful wife today also brings joy to her husband and fills his mind with peace. She is God's generous gift to him, priceless because of her unfailing love for him.

It will not always be easy for her to make herself fit into these biblical descriptions of the faithful wife. For this she needs God's help; and she must ask him for it every day. Then she will have reason to hope that God will also bless her with a faithful man who loves her as deeply as she loves him.

Chapter 31

God's Love Watches

TOBIT and ANNA   (Tobit)

A QUICK look at the Old Testament's book of Tobit (sometimes called Tobias) makes you think its story is pretty far-fetched. Closer study will dig out the precious lesson which God teaches us in this story.

Tobit, an Israelite belonging to the clan of Nephtali, lived in Galilee about 700 B.C. He married a relative named Anna who bore him a son, Tobias. This family was deported to Nineveh (near Mosul in modern Iraq) by Assyrian invaders of Galilee. At Nineveh, Tobit managed to get a good job in the court of the Assyrian king, and during this time he deposited ten talents of silver (about $7500) with a relative named Gabael who lived at Ragae (near Tehran in modern Persia).

The next Assyrian king turned out to be a Jew-hater. Tobit risked his own life many a time by giving his murdered kin a decent burial. Things got so bad that he had to leave Nineveh for a while. During his absence his property was confiscated but his wife and child were not harmed. When a new king came to the throne Tobit rejoined his family at their home in Nineveh.

But the Jews in the city were still persecuted severely, and Tobit still did everything he could to bury the victims properly. One night after returning from a secret funeral, he was sleeping in the open courtyard of his home when some bird dung fell into his eyes and blinded him. Because of this and other troubles he became so discouraged that he prayed God to let him die. Then he remembered the money he had left with Gabael, and he asked his son to go and get it. When a companion was sought for young Tobias, a certain Raphael, who later turned out to be an angel of God, presented himself for the job. When Tobit questioned him about his family background the angel told Tobit he was a relative of his and that his name was Azariah. With this assurance Tobit hired Raphael to make the trip with his son.

When Raphael and young Tobias set out for Ragae, Tobit and Anna began the long wait for their son's return. Finally he did come back, with the money and a wife. And after he had restored his father's sight by smearing his eyes with the gall of a fish which Raphael had helped him to catch, there was much happy celebrating all around. When Tobit and his son tried to pay Raphael for his excellent services, he told them that he was God's angel and that he had been sent by God to help them. At this news the two men fell flat on their faces, and Raphael had to tell them not to be afraid. When they got up he was gone, and old Tobit's joy broke out in a flood of praise to God, who had been so good to him.

The last days of Tobit and Anna were bright with happiness. They loved their daughter-in-law Sarah and were immensely pleased that she was the wife of their son. They grew old proudly watching the young family grow. When they died, Tobias gave them them a fine funeral; then he and his wife and children moved to Ecbatana, her home city.

A few lines cannot say all that the sacred author was trying to teach us in this story. One big truth which his story offers is this, that the strongest support a man and his wife can have in their troubles is God. Tobit's lowest moment came when, because of his blindness, his wife had to take a job in order to make a living for the family. His male pride was hurt; he became extremely sensitive and irritable, and prayed God to let him die. It was at this point that he remembered the money again and sent his son to get it. This was money he had earned and it should be used to support the family rather than the money that came in from his wife's job. Anna's worst days came during the long wait for her son's return home; she lost many a tear over him and at times she almost gave up hope of ever seeing him again. But in all these troubles which at times made them quarrel bitterly they kept trusting in God.

In real life a couple's trust in God is not always rewarded as soon as Tobit's and Anna's was. A husband and father may be physically handicapped, may be blinded for example, with never a son of his to smear the gall of a fish on his eyes and cure him. His patience and humility may be tested even more severely than Tobit's when he has to see family expenses defrayed at least in part by the work of his wife or children, people whom he wants to support by his own work but cannot. He needs an even greater trust in God than Tobit.

A woman in Anna's shoes may have an even harder task than hers when she has not only a woman's work but also a man's work to do. She may also have to wait for the return of a son or daughter. She may shed more tears than Anna, especially if she is waiting for her child to return not from a distant city back to the home town, but back to God. She will find herself saying with Anna, "The child has perished; that is why he takes so long." She will go on thinking so until God some day shows her that her trust in him was not misplaced.

Many biblical scholars today, Catholics and non-Catholics, think that the literary form to which the book of Tobit belongs is something like the modern historical novel. We will come close to an understanding of the sacred writer's meaning if we look for the truth, not in the detailed events which he narrates, but in the picture of human life which shows up in these events and in the writer's interpretation of life. Tobit and Anna trusted God in all their troubles; and although through human weakness they sometimes quarreled and lost heart and came near to despair, in the end they found happiness. And they knew that somehow it came from God.

Chapter 32

A Daughter's Wedding

RAGUEL and EDNA (Tobit)

IN the story told by the Old Testament's book of Tobit a Jewish couple, Raguel and Edna, lived in Ecbatana (near Tehran in modern Iran) with their only daughter Sarah.

A strange problem had developed in this family. Sarah, a beautiful and intelligent girl, had attempted marriage several times; but each time, before the marriage bed was used, her husband mysteriously died. Sarah herself had done nothing to cause these deaths; she was, in fact so distressed over the whole thing that she found herself thinking about suicide.

Alone at her window, Sarah begged God either to let her die or else to show her some pity and do something to change the situation that was spoiling her life. Although Sarah seems to have had no idea what the trouble was, the author of the story points to the demon Asmodaeus as the killer of Sarah's husbands. Later in the story young Tobias seems to think that this demon was somehow in love with the girl and was killing her husbands out of jealousy.

All this sounds very strange; and strange things are to follow in the story. Tobit's son, Tobias, was on his way with unrecognized angel Raphael to pick up some money which his father had deposited with a relative. As the two approached Ecbatana, Raphael told Tobias about Sarah.

Although their families were kin, Tobias knew Sarah only by hearsay.

Raphael told Tobias that he ought to marry Sarah on their way back home through Ecbatana, and he began to praise her beauty and intelligence. Tobias then reminded Raphael of stories he had heard about the death of Sarah's husbands, a point which Raphael had not mentioned. Tobias feared that he too would be struck dead if he married Sarah, so he was not altogether satisfied with the angel's match-making.

Raphael insisted that Tobias should go ahead and marry her, and gave him instructions on how to make the demon Asmodaeus leave her for good. He was to take the heart and liver of a fish, which Rapheal had helped him to catch, and was to burn them in the marriage bedroom; when the demon smelled the burning stuff he would have to leave and would never come near Sarah again.

Raphael promised Tobias that if he followed these directions he would get himself a wonderful wife and would not be harmed in any way by the demon who had killed her other husbands. When the angel began to speak of the children the happy couple would have, Tobias found himself falling in love with Sarah.

The travelers got a warm welcome at Raguel's home. When Tobias had told how things were going with his father and mother back in Nineveh, he asked Raphael to bring up the subject of the marriage. The angel did so, and Raguel agreed to give his daughter to Tobias. But he felt obliged to tell the young man about the sad fate of Sarah's other husbands.

"Eat, drink, and be merry. You are the one to take my child as a wife. But I must tell you the truth. I have given my child to seven husbands. And each time one would approach her he died during the night. Still, be merry now."

In spite of the ominous warning, Tobias didn't want to wait for the return trip through Ecbatana as Raphael had planned, but married Sarah then and there. Raguel gave his daughter to her new husband, blessed them, and saw that the contract of marriage was written and sealed. Then they all ate.

Later when Edna had made the marriage bedroom ready, both mother and daughter began to cry; they were dreading another mysterious death to turn their joy into grief again. Edna tried to cheer her child. "Cheer up, child! May the LORD of heaven and earth give you joy in place of this sorrow. Cheer up, daughter!" Then Sarah waited for her husband.

When Tobias entered the room he burned the heart and liver of the fish as Raphael had told him. The demon, smelling the smoke, sped away to the farthest parts of upper Egypt where Raphael tied him up tight. Then, after praying to God, Tobias and Sarah slept.

By this time Raguel had gotten used to the sad job of burying his daughter's husbands. So he spent part of the night digging a grave for Tobias. But when the newly-weds were found sleeping and unharmed next morning, Raguel gave happy thanks to God.

"O God, you are blessed in every way. May your saints and all your creatures bless you. May your angels and your chosen ones bless you forever. . . . Blessed are you because you have shown mercy to two only children. Show them mercy, LORD, see them through life in health and happiness and mercy."

For two weeks they celebrated while Raphael went on alone to get the money for Tobias' father. After the angel returned with the money Tobias and his wife finally managed to break away from the loving company of her jubilant parents.

As they were getting ready to leave, Raguel blessed them and wished them fertility. Then after telling his daughter to look on her husband's parents as her own, he kissed her good-by. Edna said to Tobias, "Dear brother, the LORD of heaven will bring you back. May he let me see your children by my daughter Sarah, so that I may be glad in the LORD's presence. Here I give you my daughter as a precious trust. Don't grieve her, now!"

Raguel and Edna did in fact see Tobias and Sarah again with their children sometime later, after Tobias' parents had died and the decision was made to go back to Ecbatana to live. When Raguel and Edna died, Tobias gave them splendid funerals.

No one today knows just how much of the story told in the book of Tobit is fact and how much is fiction. Many scholars think that the author started with a real event and then used his imagination to build the event into a story that would make his readers aware of the values of family life.

Coming through the strangeness that pervades a story written so long ago is the recognizable picture of human life and its problems. The author has put into his story the sorrows and joys of real people. The joy of Raguel and Edna over the wedding of their daughter is lived over again every time a girl gladdens her parents by marrying a man whom they also love.

The joy which a happy marriage brings to newly-weds and to their parents is interpreted by the author of the book of Tobit as one of God's best gifts. For it God must be thanked.

Chapter 33

United in Prayer

TOBIAS and SARAH   (Tobit)

THE angel Raphael played cupid for Tobias and Sarah. In the story told by the Old Testament's book of Tobit, young Tobias and Raphael were on their way from Nineveh (near modern Mosul in Iraq) to Ragae (near Tehran in Iran) to get some money which Tobias' father had left with a relative. On the way they had to pass through Ecbatana, the home of another family related to Tobias; there Raguel and Edna lived with their only daughter Sarah.

As the travelers neared Ecbatana, Raphael spoke so warmly about Sarah's beauty and good sense that Tobias began to fall in love with her. Sarah herself was right in the center of a harrowing experience which had driven her almost to suicide. Seven times she had attempted marriage; but each time sudden death for her husband when he approached her bed on the wedding night had turned joy into tragedy.

Even when Raphael and Tobias were coming into the city Sarah had no idea what was wrong, and she was begging God either to do something about the mysterious problems or else let her die. The author of the book names the demon Asmodaeus as the killer of Sarah's husbands, and Tobias himself said that this demon was in love with Sarah and

murderously jealous of any man who loved her. But Raphael
told Tobias to marry Sarah anyway; and, in order to escape
the death that Asmodaeus had dealt to the seven men, he
advised Tobias to burn a fish's heart and liver in the wedding
bedroom. The smell of the burning fish would drive the
demon away. So, Raphael assured him, Tobias would save
Sarah from her unhappiness and would take her home
with him, and she would bear him children.

When they met, Tobias and Sarah loved each other. Soon
the wedding day came. But as that happy day was ending
Sarah and her mother began to cry when they prepared the
wedding bedroom; they felt sure that this fine young man
Tobias would die like all the others. But when he came
into the room Tobias followed Raphael's instructions about
burning the fish, and the demon left in a hurry. Then Tobias
prayed with Sarah at his side. "Blessed are you, God of our
fathers. Your holy and glorious name is blessed forever.
May the heavens and all your creatures bless you. You
made Adam and gave him his wife Eve as help and support.
The human race came from them. You said—it is not good
for man to be alone. Let us make him a helper like himself. And now, LORD, it is not with fornication in mind that
I take my sister here, but genuinely. Be sure to be merciful
to me and let me grow old with her." Sarah said amen to her
husband's prayer, and they slept without harm the whole
night.

Sarah's father, who had spent part of the night digging
a grave for his daughter's husband was surprised and immensely glad to find Tobias alive and sleeping peacefully
with Sarah when morning came. For two whole weeks
they all celebrated the wedding. Finally the happy couple
broke away from the loving company of the bride's parents
and started back to Nineveh. There they were welcomed
just as lovingly by Tobias' parents, Tobit and Anna, who

had waited so long and painfully for their son to come home. His mother's first act was to take him close in her arms and say, "I have seen you, child. Now I can die." And Tobit was just as happy over his daughter-in-law when he told her, "You come as one most welcome daughter. Blessed be God who brought you to us. And blessed be your father and mother."

Tobit had sent his son after some money and the job had been done. But young Tobias had also brought back a wonderful wife who was worth more than any amount of money. He and Sarah raised their own children at Nineveh until his parents died. Then they moved to Ecbatana where they lived until Tobias died, a very old man.

Many scholars have reason to think that the book of Tobit is a piece of fiction built around a real event for the purpose of teaching the values of family life. These values are certainly taught in the book. Tobias and Sarah were deeply aware of the fact that marriage comes from God. Sarah knew this when she begged God to help her out of the mysterious problem that was spoiling her life. Tobias knew that the joys of his union with Sarah came from God when he prayed just before they slept on his wedding night for a long life with her. The strange part about the demon Asmodaeus may have been the author's way of saying that the earlier husbands of Sarah were punished for not accepting marriage as God's gift.

Tobias did accept Sarah, and she accepted him, as God's gift. This explains their reverence for one another and their strong tender love. They both knew that God was the most important witness of their wedding, that he was present at its fulfillment on their wedding night, and that he would bless them with his love all their long life together. Without his help Tobias would have died like Sarah's other husbands, and that might have grieved Sarah enough to kill herself. With his help came joy for both of them and a full life and children. They knew what we must learn, that God is the Maker of marriage and that he is pleased with what he made.

Chapter 34

Brave Woman

MANASSEH and JUDITH   (Judith)

JUDITH was a very beautiful woman. So says the author of the Old Testament book that bears her name. She also feared God with her whole heart. Her husband, Manasseh, was a prosperous farmer. But soon after their marriage he suffered a heart stroke on his farm and died.

Judith did not marry again, although many men wanted her. Manasseh had left her plenty of money and servants and cattle and land; so she had no wants of that kind. But she missed her husband very much and stayed in mourning for a long time. During this time she fasted a great deal and prayed often to God. Everybody loved her and spoke well of her.

But the story told in the book of Judith is just beginning. Bad times had hit her home town, Bethulia. Fear of total destruction gripped all her fellow townsmen. Holofernes and his Assyrian invaders were there outside the city walls and their siege had already reduced the people of Bethulia to near madness because of the shortage of drinking water. When people came to the city's leading men and urged them to surrender rather than let the people die of thirst, an agreement was reached: they would try to hold out five days longer. At the end of that period, if God did not step in to save His people, they would surrender.

Judith heard about this five-day ultimatum which her people's leaders had handed to God, and told them that it was wrong to put God to the test in this way. The way to meet the problem, she insisted, was not to wait for God to take some spectacular action; the thing to do was to work out a plan that would destroy the Assyrian forces. Judith told them that she had such a plan and that with God's help she could make it work.

After explaining the whole thing to her amazed leaders, she went into action. Her first action was prayer; she poured her heart out to God and begged him for strength. Then she took off her widow garments, bathed and perfumed herself, fixed her hair and dressed in her best clothes—as she had done for her husband. Anklets, bracelets, rings and all her other ornaments were added. In this way, the sacred writers tells us, she "made herself very beautiful to draw the eyes of any men who would see her."

The first men to be attracted by her beauty were the leaders of her own people as they watched her walk out through the city gates with her maid. She made her way straight to the camp of Holofernes, leader of the Assyrians. When she was arrested by Assyrian guards, she asked them to take her to their leader. Now it was the guards' turn to be caught by her beauty. By the time they had taken her to Holofernes the whole camp was buzzing with the news that a Hebrew woman had come into their midst, and what a beautiful woman!

The personal attendants of the Assyrian commander were the next to admire Judith's beauty. When she came into his presence she fell on her face at his feet, and from that moment Holofernes too fell victim to her charms. She spoke to him at great length. From the start he went out of his way to be nice to her and he saw to it that no one molested her in any way. She and her maid had free run of the camp.

They all took it for granted that she was on their side, and so they trusted her without any misgivings.

On the fourth day after Judith's arrival, Holofernes invited her to be guest of honor at his banquet. She came to the banquet looking her beautiful best. This time the eye of Holofernes was not only fixed on her; his mind was set on having her for his own use that night. Holofernes invited her to drink and be merry with him, and she went into her act. He fell for her and drank so much he had to be put to bed.

A little later, the chief of Holofernes' bodyguards made everybody leave Judith alone with the Assyrian commander in his tent. Inside the tent Judith stood over the bed on which the drunken man sprawled. She made a last quick prayer to God, then grabbed the heavy sword that was hanging ready by the bed, and with two determined slashes cut Holofernes' head clean from his body. She rolled the body off the bed, pulled the canopy down over body and bed, took the head with her and gave it to her maid who dropped it into their food basket. Then the two women went through the still of night to the gates of their city.

Once inside the city, Judith told her people all that had happened, and unrestrained rejoicing broke loose. At her orders, Hebrew fighting men went out early next morning and ran straight for the Assyrian camp. When the Assyrians saw them coming they sent word to Holofernes' tent for orders to go kill these Hebrews. But when they entered their commander's tent and found his headless body and no Judith around, the chilling truth came on them. Without their leader they were utterly confused and made a disorganized retreat during which they were easy victims for the onrushing Hebrews. After destroying them and looting their camp, the Hebrew fighters returned in triumph to Bethulia where Judith and her people were waiting.

The people of Bethulia could not praise Judith enough. Judith herself entered into the crowds with her whole heart and soul. "In the wild joy of a celebration which they held in her honor, Judith led the merry-makers in song and dance." Judith, in words that ring with the intoxication of her victory, gave credit to God for it all. The victory celebration took them to Jerusalem where they worshipped God in his temple.

Then Judith went back to Bethulia where she lived on her own estate, well loved and honored by all. She died at the age of 105 and was buried beside her husband Manasseh.

The sacred author, and God who speaks to us through him, did not write this story just for the sake of preserving a record of events. In fact, there are good reasons for regarding the book of Judith, not as a record of events, but as a piece of fiction built up around Israel's history. But as we read the book we become aware of the author's faith in God's loving providence and care for his people. And the episode of Judith and Holofernes can be seen as a kind of symbol of the whole history of God's chosen people. Many times God used unlikely means—such as the woman Judith—to save his people from threatening evils.

What can Christian wives learn from the story of Judith? As they read, will they not see that they too must often summon up a courage similar to Judith's? True, they don't ordinarily have to do anything quite so violent. But courage like Judith's is needed to meet trying situations more often than once in 105 years. Will they not also approve and share the conviction she showed when she learned of the way her leaders expected God to take some spectacular step to save them? Will they not agree that what is required is not a tranquil waiting for God to act, but rather the use of one's brains in planning how to meet problems, and vigor in putting these plans into effect—all the while praying and trusting that God will see the plans through to a successful end?

The feminine courage which saved Bethulia from Holofernes can be found today in the heart of many a woman whose brains and hard work and love are the means by which God saves her family from evil and blesses all its members. To her we may say what the people of Bethulia said to Judith, "Your hand has done all this. All this good you have done with Israel—and you, O God, are well pleased by it all." And she will learn to sing in her heart the song of Judith, "I will sing my God a new song. LORD, you are great and glorious, wonderfully strong, unconquerable."

Chapter 35

Life Risked for Her People

XERXES and ESTHER (Esther)

ARLY in the fifth century before Christ, a huge beauty contest was announced in Shushan, Persia. Girls out of all the Persian provinces from India to Ethiopia started coming to the harem of King Xerxes I to compete. First place depended on the vote of one man, the king, who was looking for a new queen among all these beauties. His former queen, Vashti, had been dethroned because she refused to expose her beauty to the wine-soaked cronies of her husband.

Each of the girls who entered the contest spent twelve months prettying herself for her meeting with the king. Then each girl in turn passed a night with him and so became his concubine. On the basis of his association with her on that night the king was to decide whether a particular girl was to be his queen or just another number in his harem.

Among the contestants was a Jewess named Hadassah, but better known as Esther, which is also the title of the Old Testament book which tells her story. After the death of her parents she was raised by a devoted uncle, Mordecai. He wanted his beautiful niece to try to become the new queen because of his concern for the Jewish people living in the Persian empire. If a Jewess could be queen of all

Persia, her kin would not only be relieved of the threat of persecution but also assured of royal favors.

So without letting the king know of her Jewish blood, Esther took her place among the other girls and eventually spent her night with the king. She pleased him so well that he declared an end to the contest. Xerxes had found his queen. The king loved her more than all his other wives. And he made her his queen in place of Vashti.

Meantime Mordecai, whose Jewish blood was known to all, had refused to bow and scrape to Haman, who was the king's high-handed vizier. Haman was so irked by Mordecai's attitude that he planned a vast persecution of the Jews throughout the Persian empire. King Xerxes, without paying much attention to the affair approved Haman's plan and authorized a massacre of the Jews scheduled for the 13th of the month Adar (February-March). When Mordecai learned about Haman's plan, he saw at once that Esther was the only person who might be able to change the king's mind.

Considering the king's petulance as shown in his dismissal of Queen Vashti, Esther knew that her task was full of danger. But when Mordecai convinced her that she was her people's only hope, she made her plan. First she invited the king and Haman to a banquet set for the following day. Haman was delighted at the invitation, but on his way home he was violently upset again at the sight of Mordecai. This time his anger pushed him to prepare a gallows on which he would hang the stubborn Jew next day if he could get the king's permission.

The night before the banquet King Xerxes had a dream about Mordecai; and after checking his chronicle he found that Mordecai had once done him the favor of saving his life. Xerxes then decided he must do something to honor the Jew. When Haman came next morning to ask the king's permission to hang Mordecai, the king spoke first. "What will I do for the man whom I wish to honor?" Haman thought the king was referring to him; so he began to count off the various honors he hoped the king would grant him. At the end of Haman's long list of suggestions the king told him to go and confer these honors on the Jew Mordecai. Sick with disgust, Haman carried out the king's orders and then went home to sulk. Soon a messenger came to escort him to Queen Esther's banquet; there was nothing he could do but go. During the banquet King Xerxes told his queen, "What is it, Queen Esther? What sign of honor do you ask? It will be yours even if it is half of my kingdom."

With her king in such a frame of mind Esther saw that it was time for her to act. She told him that she was a Jewess and that Haman, who was sitting there with them at the table, was the malicious mind that had planned the massacre of all the Jews in the Persian empire. When Xerxes' angry eyes turned on him, Haman knew he was doomed and himself begged Queen Esther to spare his life. But the next moment Haman was hanging on the gallows which he had prepared for Mordecai. Mordecai then took Haman's place as the king's vizier, and quick action was taken to revoke the decree of massacre and to send out another decree giving the Jews permission to kill their enemies on the 13th day of Adar. When this day came the Jews of Shushan killed their enemies in the city; and at Esther's request the ten sons of Haman were also hanged. So after these remarkable reversals of plan, the Jews of Persia were saved from destruction and rose high in the favor of King Xerxes. Mordecai's plan for Esther had been a success; she was a new savior of her people.

It is not easy to say what was God's purpose in inspiring the author of this story, which contains several elements indicating that it is largely fictional in its details. The main truth expressed by the author is the fact that evil plans against God's chosen people sometimes turn back on the planners to punish and utterly confuse them. Outstanding also is the idea that the agent of such reversals of plan is sometimes a very unlikely one; in this case a weak woman against the strong and merciless Haman. An inspired addition to the original story tells us that unpredictable human events are really a part of God's providence in the world. Awareness of the fact that God is Lord of human history, no matter how uncontrollable that history often seems to be, is as important for us as it was for the first readers of the book of Esther.

Then too, whatever core of fact there may be in the actual sequence of events narrated in this book, the author must have known real women like the woman of his story—beautiful, clever, motivated by a sense of justice for the oppressed, daring and determined. The modern woman who admires these qualities in Esther will want them also for herself. Is it unreasonable to think that God continues to save and bless us all through such women?

Chapter 36

Man Tested by Suffering

JOB and WIFE (Job)

A SUCCESSFUL man widely known for his simple goodness towards other people and for his reverence towards God, that was Job. His wife had given him seven sons
and three daughters, and they were a happy family. But
trouble came to this family, and it came fast and hard.

First Job's property. One day almost all his cows and
donkeys and camels were rustled away and his servants killed.
The animals which had been left behind by the rustlers, and
the remaining servants who were tending them, were all
killed by lightening. While Job was listening to the man who
had brought him this sad news, another came with sadder
still. All Job's sons and daughters had just been killed when
a windstorm from the desert crushed and ground down the
home of his oldest son where they were all having a party.

Although he was deeply shaken by all this, Job managed
to accept it as the will of God somehow. "The LORD gave
and the LORD has taken away; blessed be the name of
the LORD." Job would not allow his grief over the loss
of his property and children to make him think that God
didn't know or didn't care what was happening to him.

Soon after this, Job found himself breaking out with a
repulsive skin disease that would not clear up. At this

point Job's wife snapped under the strain and yelled at him, "Curse God and die!" All alone now without even his wife to encourage him, Job still held on to his reverence for God. "Are even you going to speak as senseless women do? We accept good things from God; and should we not accept evil?"

But in spite of his effort to accept God's mysterious will, Job's troubles became a puzzle to torment his mind. Like millions of others, Job wondered why these things were happening to him. What had he done to deserve such a string of crushing blows? Of course he had sinned some, but he was not aware of having offended God seriously enough to get all this suffering loaded on him. The puzzzle bothered him so much that he too broke under its weight and hated the very fact that he was living. "Why did I not perish at birth, come forth from the womb and expire? Or why was I not buried away like an untimely birth, like babes that have never seen the light? Wherefore did the knees receive me? Or why did I suck at the breasts?" He had reached the point where he was thinking that death was better than life. Maybe his wife was right after all. Maybe he should curse God and die.

Three of Job's friends came to comfort him. But their comfort misfired. They kept telling him that if he would only acknowledge his secret serious crime—which they said he must be guilty of to deserve such suffering—God would restore his health and family and property and would make everything right again. But Job told them that he had no such crime to own up to. They insisted he must have; otherwise God would be unjust. Job said no he hadn't. And there they all stand. Nothing is accomplished, except that Job gets more and more impatient with them and tells them to shut up and leave him alone.

A stranger enters the argument and tells Job's friends

that their advice is worthless. Then he turns to Job and blames him for demanding an explanation from God, for acting as if God had an obligation to make everything perfectly clear to him.

Finally, God himself speaks out of a storm and convinces Job that he ought to take his place alongside the mountain goats and wild asses and ostriches and horses and hippopotamuses and all the other creatures. All of them are subject to a mysterious and careful plan of God which neither they nor any man understands completely. Why should not Job, in spite of his troubles, accept the fact of God's careful loving plan for him too, even if he can't understand it very well?

Job sees his mistake and accepts the fact of God's plan, and he submits himself to all of it by withdrawing his demand for an explanation. He had been on the right track in the first place, but the pain had confused him. "We accept good things from God; and should we not accept evil?" There can be a reason even for the evil, and God can know what that reason is. Job no longer thinks that he has to know. It is enough for God to know.

But once he had made up his mind to live with the trouble, it all goes away. Job gets well. His property is soon twice what it was before. His wife bears him seven more sons and three daughters to take the place of the first ten. "After this, Job lived a hundred and forty years; and he saw his children, his grandchildren, and even his great-grandchildren. Then Job died old and full of years."

The Old Testament's book of Job, which tells this story, is not only a masterpiece of Hebrew literature but also a part of the inspired word of God to Christians. The author has taken as his starting point a tradition of 5th century B.C. Palestine about a man who continued, in spite of great misfortunes, to believe in God's wisdom and goodness. Most of the details of the story of Job are intentionally fictitious. They serve to intensify the problem which filled the mind of the author. The problem is: how is a person to go on believing in the wisdom and goodness of God when he sees all around him and experiences in his own life evils which seem to contradict God's wisdom and goodness?

The author of Job does not pretend to give us a satisfying answer to the question which he asks. But he does give us a healthy way of thinking about the problem. And he succeeds in making us suspect that we do not need a satisfying answer and that in any case we have no right to one. The answer which he seems to give, namely the restoration of Job's property and family and health, is really no answer at all, because it doesn't explain why God allowed the loss of these things in the first place. But by making us aware of our close kinship with all other creatures, the author prepares us to accept the fact that God's wisdom and goodness seen in earth and sky and water, in the breeding of the mountain goats and in the soaring of a hawk, are also at work in the life of men and women. And if this is true, then even the loss of property and family and health can be accepted as somehow fitting into God's wisdom and goodness.

The New Testament teaching about original sin and about life after death has done much to clarify for us some of the problem of evil. More than anything else, the love of Christ suffering and dying on the cross has shown us that God can have an excellent reason for allowing men to suffer. This does not mean that we have stopped feeling grief and pain. Christ, who knew perfectly well the excellent reason behind his grief and pain on the cross, still cried out, "My God, my God, why have you abandoned me!" But the grief and pain which we experience will not drive us to bitterness. They will be seen as the problematical part of God's love.

Husband and wives today, as well as those who lived in the 5th century before Christ, need to learn to think along the lines of the book of Job. A sense of closeness and likeness to all other creatures, an awareness of being a part of God's world and therefore an object of God's loving concern, a willingness to accept unavoidable evil along with the good—all this belongs in the mentality of husbands and wives today. "The LORD gave and the LORD has taken away; blessed be the name of the LORD." These words of Job will come to their lips, not easily maybe, but not grudgingly either.

PART FIVE

Time of Christ

Chapter 37

Faithful to God

ZACHARY and ELIZABETH   (Luke 1)

IN the Old Testament way of looking at the realities of human life, having children—as many as possible—was not automatically a sign of God's love. But in the ordinary run of events, that was the nearest thing to a sign of God's love that a husband and his wife could get. Being without children was not automatically a sign of God's displeasure either. But many Hebrew believers thought it was.

If a man and his wife were making honest efforts to do God's will as it was known to them through the law of Moses, they considered themselves eligible for the blessings promised by God to such people. The book of Deuteronomy promised them, "The LORD will increase in more than goodly measure the fruit of your womb." If this promised blessing was not given, the fact that a married couple would continue to make efforts to do God's will was something of a wonder.

Saint Luke shares this wonder with us when he describes Zachary and Elizabeth. "They were both just before God, living in full obedience to the LORD'S just commands— they were blameless. But they had no child, since Elizabeth was sterile, and they were both well along in years." They obeyed God, but they had no child.

Why did they obey him? Not for the reward of obedience, since the thing they wanted most had been denied them. Before Christ had taught his apostles about life after death, people were not in the habit of thinking about an eternal reward for obedience to God. Zachary and Elizabeth went on serving God because, as they knew, God has a right to be served. It was love for God and not any advantage for themselves that urged them to go on year after childless year faithful to God.

Both of them, especially Zachary, had in the earlier years of their marriage prayed to God for that first child. Saint Luke's description of what happened next seems to say that they were still praying for a child. But if they were, this prayer at least on Zachary's part was not a bit hopeful. He considered both himself and his wife to be too old ever to have a child now. How old is old? Saint Luke leaves us lots of room here. Did he mean they were about 80? or 50? We don't know. At any rate, when God answered their hopeless prayer, the birth of little John is rightly seen as a miracle of God's goodness to them.

Saint Luke draws a clear picture. While Zachary was performing his priestly duties in the Jerusalem temple, God's messenger Gabriel told him that Elizabeth was soon going to bear him a son whom he was to call John. Zachary didn't believe a word of it, and in punishment for his disbelief he was unable to speak until the child was born and circumcised.

When Elizabeth knew that she was carrying a baby she was ecstatic with the joy of her pregnancy. "This is what the LORD has done for me in the days when he took away my reproach in the eyes of men." Her joy, and little John's joy, broke out again when Elizabeth's much younger cousin, who had become pregnant in a still more remarkable way, came from Nazareth to visit her and to help her in her confinement. "How did I get this favor of having the mother of my LORD come to me? Just now, as the sound of your greeting met my ears, the child in my womb leaped for joy."

Zachary found his voice again on the day they circumcised their eight-day-old child. And for the day he was the happiest man in the world. Long before this boy's teaching mission would begin in the desert of Juda, little John had taught his father one thing just by lying there with his mother. Zachary and Elizabeth were definitely not too old to have a child; God was unpredictable.

This first part of Saint Luke's good news has made it possible for all believers to share the joy of Elizabeth and Zachary. "Her neighbors and relatives heard that the LORD had shown his great mercy to her, and they congratulated her."

By reading the first chapter of Saint Luke's gospel carefully, husbands and wives today can learn an important lesson about their own relationship with God. Even though the signs of God's love for all of us are many and very powerful, for various reasons they are not always easy to see. The problem may be the very one that troubled Zachary and Elizabeth, that first baby still longed for and nowhere in sight. Or the very opposite; it may be the difficulty of taking care of so many children. Long and expensive sickness, various reasons for disappointment with themselves or their children—such things can become a source of discouragement and so can make it hard for husbands and wives to go on serving God faithfully.

At such times you need the spirit of Zachary and Elizabeth, who served God mainly because he has a right to be served, and not only because he rewards those who serve him. If we are too eager for rewards, especially the rewards we pick for ourselves and set our hearts on, we are bound to suffer discouragement when we don't see them coming our way. But if we try to serve God mainly because we love him and because he has a right to our service, and not only because we love ourselves and hope to win his rewards, discouragement will not be a big threat to our relationship with God.

Gradually we learn that having God is having infinitely more than anything else God could give us. And there is always the possibility that he will surprise us as he did the parents of John the Baptist by giving us what we had almost stopped hoping for. God does not change. He is still unpredictable.

Chapter 38

Old Woman at Prayer

ANNA and HUSBAND (Luke 2)

EVEN casual readers of popular magazines know that there is a lot of busy work going on these days among scholars —Catholics as well as others—who are studying the New Testament. Some people are shocked when they hear their fellow believers calling into question their traditional ideas about the meaning of certain passages in the gospels. The public is becoming aware of the activity of its scholars. The best of these scholars often say that their work is far from finished and that their duty is to continue sound methods of study in order to arrive at correct interpretations of the biblical texts.

The gospel passages that tell the story of Christ's infancy, Matthew 1-2 and Luke 1-2, are being studied more carefully than ever before. And a question is becoming more urgent in many minds: What are these inspired writers telling us? Without losing sight of the core of fact, namely the birth of Christ, one may wonder how much of the detail offered by these accounts was intended by the inspired writers to be factual and how much of it they intended as having a function different from a simple telling of fact. At present nobody has a satisfying answer to this question.

We're not going to try to find the answer here. But it

seems important to ask the question and to keep it in mind while we look at the story of Anna in Luke 2, 36-38. What did the inspired writer mean to tell when he put down this text and what is its value for us today? What was his attitude towards this woman and what can we learn from his description?

Luke's gospel tells that on the 40th day after Christ's birth Joseph and Mary presented him in the temple and offered the sacrifice of two doves according to the Jewish law. The old man Simeon was there to take the child in his arms and to rejoice over the fact that at long last he had seen the Messiah. An old woman was there too. Her name was Anna, and she is called a prophet, which means that she was recognized as a wise woman who could speak in God's name to others or represent others in prayer to God. Long ago as a girl she had married; but after seven years of marriage her husband died, and she remained a widow. Now in her 84th year, she spent most of her time in the temple at Jerusalem praying to God and fasting a great deal. There in the temple, at the very time when Joseph and Mary were busy with the presentation ceremony, Anna was talking to her fellow Jews about the Messiah, the long expected leader of the Jewish people.

The gospel text, although it puts down many details about Anna's family and age and religious activity, is vague about the connection between her and the holy family there in the temple. Luke does not say whether she talked to them, whether she recognized, as Simeon did, the Messiah in Mary's arms. So we can't say either. The fact that she was in the habit of praying and fasting while she waited for the Messiah shows that she was not among those who expected him to be a military leader only. Rather she belongs to that smaller company who knew that the Messiah would save his people from their sins rather than from the Romans.

Luke makes only a passing reference to Anna's marriage so many years before, and he says nothing about any children who might have been born in this family. What value does this text have for us today? The inspired writer—and God who inspired him—gives beautiful expression to his respect for an old woman who prays. Today in many churches and in many homes there are old women who pray. They do this without making a big show of what they are doing, sometimes making a real sacrifice to walk to church for Mass and holy Communion during the week. Sometimes they are called by God to make the greater sacrifice of feeling that they are useless or even a burden on those who must take care of them. Their patience and their silent prayer to God goes on and on. Some of them are widows like Anna, for long years remembering a husband who is no longer in the house. Their prayers and sacrifices, their love for God and their patience in waiting for him to come, their desire to help others in whatever way they can—surely Anna of Luke's gospel reminds us of all this.

Sometimes these praying women become the objects of jokes to busy bodies whose shallow minds are amused by the sight of them. But if we are supposed to live in an attitude of prayer in obedience to Christ's command that we should pray always, then these women have nothing to be embarrassed about when others express amusement over them. God takes them to his heart along with their prayers, and what they are doing can have an effect on us all. Some of them have been praying relentlessly for the return of a son or daughter to the practice of religion or for health or job or for the ability to carry crosses without bitterness. And sometimes their prayers are answered.

In his encyclical on the Mystical Body of Christ in 1943 Pope Pius XII insisted on the vital importance of such people as these modern Annas and their prayers in the life of the Church. The Pope gives a severe correction to those who make light of private prayer in their efforts to show the greater value of the Church's public prayer. "There are others who ... would spread abroad the idea that prayers offered to God in private should not be considered worth very much. Public prayers, they say, prayers that are made in the name of the Church, are those which really count, as they come from the Mystical Body of Jesus Christ. Such an opinion is false; for the Divine Redeemer maintains closest union not only with his Church, which is his loved spouse, but also with each and every faithful soul in it, and he longs to speak with them heart to heart, especially after holy Communion. It is true that public prayers, prayers, that is, that are offered by Mother Church, because of the dignity of the spouse of Christ, excel any other kind of prayer; but no prayer, even the most private, lacks its own dignity and power, and all prayer is immensely helpful to the Mystical Body."

These words of Pope Pius XII, which express the gospel teaching of Christ about prayer, should encourage the praying women to keep up their good work and not to let us down. And maybe even before we get to be 84 years old we will learn to follow their example.

Chapter 39

Presence of Christ

HUSBAND and WIFE at CANA   (John 2)

JOHN, who is the only gospel writer to tell about the wedding at Cana, doesn't give the names of the bride and groom and doesn't even refer expressly to the bride. John's interest centers on the presence of another woman at the wedding party.

Mary, the mother of Jesus, was there by special invitation. Jesus, who was not living with his mother any more, was also asked to come. After he arrived with several of his followers, the wine supply began to run low. Mary saw the situation, became concerned and mentioned the problem to her son.

Many questions are raised by the way in which John describes this give-and-take between mother and son. Did she or didn't she ask him to work a miracle? Did he or didn't he refuse something to her even while he worked the miracle? Although the main drift of the passage is clear, these questions have never been fully answered—and we're not trying to answer them now. Another question is more urgent—Does the wedding at Cana have any meaning for husbands and wives today?

At Cana Jesus changed water into wine. Modern readers of the gospels may tend to think that the miracles of Jesus are totally foreign to their own experience. And this strangeness may even be the source of inner uneasiness and of a tendency to disbelief. Saint Augustine faced this problem when he talked to his African Christians over fifteen centuries ago. His remarks about the miracle at Cana can help us today. He can show us that we are witness of still greater miracles worked by the same Jesus Christ who loved the newlyweds at Cana and helped them out of an embarrassing moment so that the joy of their wedding might not be lessened by a shortage of wine.

"The miracle worked by our Lord Jesus Christ when he made wine out of water is not astonishing to those who know that it was God who did it. Who was the person who made wine that day at the wedding in those six jars? It was the very one who does this same thing every year in the vines! What the waiters put into the jars turned into wine by the work of the Lord. So too, what the clouds pour down is changed into wine by the work of the same Lord. But we don't get excited about this, because it happens every year. By reason of its regularity, this change of water into wine has lost its hold on our wonder. But it really deserves more attention than the change which took place in the water jars. If anybody thinks about the activity of God ruling and taking care of this whole world, isn't such a thinker stunned and overwhelmed by wonders? If he just considers the power in one grain of seed, it becomes a great and awesome thing to him. But because men are intent on other aspects of reality and so have lost the habit of thinking about God's activity—if they did think about it they would praise the Creator every day—God has kept in reserve some unusual things to do. And he does them in order to wake up sleepers to worship him with a sense of wonder."

If we can share this mentality of Saint Augustine, the miracle of Christ at Cana will not seem strange to us. The wine at Cana that was water before will be seen as one sign among so many others that we see every day—a sign of his love for us. In his comments on the miracle at Cana, Saint Augustine keeps reminding us that this is a wedding. The love of a man and his wife, expressed by complete physical union and resulting in the origin of new human life—this is the still greater miracle of Cana. And like the miracle of water changing into wine, the birth of a child happens so often and so regularly that many people are not moved by it. Saint Augustine said, "A dead man rises, and people are amazed. So many are born every day, and nobody gets excited. If we consider the matter carefully, it is a greater miracle for somebody to live who never lived before than for somebody who lived before to live again."

The presence of Jesus and Mary at Cana and their glad sharing of the wedding joy—what does this mean? It strengthens the message of the Old Testament's Song of Songs and of so many other Old Testament wisdom books. The love of a man for a woman, stabilized by marriage and expressed by physical union, is one of the master works of the Creator and one of the most excellent goods available to men and women. For various reasons the impression persists in some minds that this is really not so, that human love expressed through sex is somehow not a work of God and is somehow a kind of evil thing for man. Saint John's second chapter, where he tells about Jesus and Mary at the wedding in Cana, should be enough to set anyone straight on this vital subject. And the consequences of these two opposing mentalities are great indeed.

But the Catholic Church is not content with reminding us of the fact that her founder approved of marriage. The Church teaches that Jesus made marriage into a sacrament. We do not know when he did this or how. But the Church, whose teaching comes from the apostles, is convinced that he did it. This means that the marriage of two baptized persons is a source of supernatural life to their souls, the life which is their knowledge of the Father and the Son and the Holy Spirit dwelling within them, the life which is their love for the three divine Persons. The rich reality of this sacrament is open to those who have received and who are using the gift of faith. Like the water of baptism and the bread and wine on the altar at Mass, the union of a husband and his wife is something sacred and life-giving in a supernatural way. God uses their union—spiritual and physical—to signify and to bring about the more perfect union of the Church with Christ.

As Jesus changed water into wine at Cana, so today he changes the union of husband and wife—without removing any of its natural goodness and beauty and joy—into a sacrament that produces a higher kind of life for their souls even as it produces new human life from and in their bodies.

Cana is not only a town in Palestine which cannot be located with certainty. Cana is wherever there is a marriage to which Jesus and his mother are invited.

Chapter 40

A Live Daughter

JAIRUS and WIFE   (Mark 5)

O NCE in a crowd of people on the shore of Lake Galilee a man named Jairus hurried up to Christ with an urgent request. "My little daughter is dying. If only you will come and place your hands on her, so that she may be saved and may live." On their way to see the sick girl somebody came and told Jairus that she had just died, and he was about to tell Christ not to bother to come any farther.

But Jesus told him, "Don't be afraid. Just keep on believing." When they reached the house they heard the wailing of the mourners who had come to start the wake. Jesus broke up their weeping. "Why all this noise and weeping? The child has not died. She is sleeping." When they laughed at him for saying this, he put them all out of the room and took three of his apostles along with the girl's parents into the room where she lay. Then he took her by the hand and said, "Little girl, I tell you, get up!" She obeyed him; she got up and walked around. For a while her parents were so bewildered by their delight at having her alive and well that they overlooked a simple need. Jesus reminded them that she was hungry and should have something to eat.

Three of the New Testament's gospels record this event,

and if you read the accounts carefully some questions will form in your mind. Did the little girl die? At first sight the gospels don't seem to make this clear. Her father was sure that she was on the point of death, and when he got word that she had died he believed it. The mourners who started the wake were sure that she was dead. But Christ said some strange things. He said that she was not dead but only asleep. What did he mean? Was he saying that they had all really mistaken a coma for death, that she was not absolutely dead in the sense that her body was finally incapable of receiving the life-giving influence of her soul, but symptomatically dead in the sense that there were no observable signs of life in her, such as breathing or heartbeat? The circumstances make this meaning of Christ's words unlikely. On another occasion he would speak of the death of Lazarus as sleep. He means that even though Jairus' daughter was actually dead, she was really only asleep to him since he could raise the dead as easily as anyone can raise a sleeping child.

Jairus knew that their twelve-year-old daughter was alive again and walking and eating there with them only because Jesus—who had said she was not dead but only asleep— took her by the hand and told her to wake up. They could not wake her up. But he had done it that day when she was lifeless as they had done it countless times before when she was full of life. So he was the wonderful Giver of life whom they could thank every time they looked at the wonder which was their child. Over twelve years before Christ's visit to their home, Jairus and his wife had loved each other physically; and the fruit of their love was a daughter, a brand-new human person, a little girl who became a dear joy to them for twelve years. Then she was sick, and dying, and lifeless. But Jesus had come and held her hand and awakened her; and now she was alive and well, a dearer joy than ever before. To him they owed the miracle of her young life.

Husbands and wives today may miss the full meaning of this passage of the gospel. When they read it, they admire Christ for his power and even more for his loving concern about Jairus' family. But they might also conclude that this wonderful event is a far cry from anything their own family has ever experienced. The miracle of that little girl's life may be interesting, even moving, but it does not affect in any deep way the relationship of their own family to Christ.

But look a little more carefully. Isn't the origin of a new human life through the love of a man and a woman for each other always a miracle, a fact which stirs wonder in any mind that sees what has really happened? Must not the Creator be at the source of this masterpiece every time it bursts into being? And Jesus is the Creator! Can anyone but God produce a human soul, or design that marvelous complexity which is the human body with its ability to produce new human life? And Jesus is God who does this each time it happens. This miracle of conception happens so often that we can get into the habit of taking it for granted like the miracle of air and earth and water. By taking it for granted we can fail to recognize it as a miracle worked by the same divine Person who raised the daughter of Jairus from her bed.

When that little girl opened her eyes to Christ, she was looking at the very Person who had given her life in her mother's womb. She would some day have a chance to thank him not only for restoring her life but for giving it to her in the first place. Her parents too would see that this Person who had answered Jairus' urgent call for help had been present with his divine power when this little girl first began to be the fruit of their love. If he could be praised and thanked and loved for giving her back to them, he had a right to all these things for having given her to them in the first place. The second miracle was not greater than the first one. Beginning to live after never having lived before is surely no less wonderful than living again after one has already been alive before.

Thinking along these lines will help husbands and wives to see that this miracle worked by Christ for Jairus and his family is by no means an event unrelated to their own experience. They will see more clearly than before that their own mutual love and desire which urges them to complete bodily union and results in the miracle of a son or daughter—is a vital concern of Christ. They will learn that Christ is not only present in heaven and in church but also in their home, in that sacred place where their love is fruitful along with his. Their wonder and their love for him will be like the wonder and love which he stirred in the hearts of Jairus and his wife by giving them back their daughter.

Such a frame of mind does not come automatically. It requires some thought. But neither is it beyond the capability of Christians today. The treasure is there in the gospels waiting to be dug up.

Chapter 41

Keeping the Door Open

THE SAMARITAN DIVORCEE   (John 4)

CHRIST was tired from the long walk that had brought him and his disciples to the well of Jacob near the Samaritan city of Sychar in central Palestine. He sat down at the well to rest while they went into town to buy some food.

While he was resting a Samaritan woman came out to the well to fill her pitcher with water. She was surprised when he asked her to give him a drink. After all, this was a public place and she was a woman, a Samaritan woman at that, and everybody knew that it was a long standing custom of Jews and Samaritans to hate one another. Here was a Jew treating her as if he had never heard of this custom, and as if he didn't know that a meeting of this kind could arouse suspicion.

In the long conversation which followed his refreshing drink, Christ asked her to go and get her husband and then come back to the well. When she lied by telling him that she had no husband, Christ quipped, "You spoke well when you said you have no husband. You have had five men, and the man you have now is not your husband. You have told the truth." He went on to tell her a great deal about himself, and she became his willing apostle by announcing him to her people. And in spite of the Jewish-Samaritan feud, her people accepted him as their Messiah Savior.

In the minds of many of us the men and women who figure in the gospels never quite take on the flesh and blood and bone of real people. But after a good hard look at chapter 4 of Saint John's gospel where the conversation of Christ and the Samaritan woman is given we will know that this woman has to be called a multiple-divorcee.

Among many intriguing aspects of this meeting, the most instructive is the simple fact that the meeting happened and that the long conversation was started and continued by Christ. He asked this disreputable woman for a drink of water, spoke to her at length about the way one ought to worship God, explained to her that he himself was the Messiah expected by her people as well as the Jews, allowed her to be his instrument in winning over her people to his person. He did all this as if she were not the kind of woman whom no respectable man would care to be seen with in public. And he knew all about her; it was not as if he mistook her for a fine upstanding woman. All very strange indeed. He didn't even lecture her for her five divorces, although he did remind her of them and in a very simple way indicated that she was not what she ought to be. They talked on and on, and somehow she was not overawed by him even when she began to see his greatness.

Saint John says that, when the disciples came back to the well, they were surprised to see Christ talking with a woman, although they had the sense not to question him about her. When they had to remind him to eat some of the food which they had bought in the town, he puzzled them by telling them that he had just eaten a very good kind of food. They took him literally and wondered if maybe the woman had given him something to eat. So he explained that the food he had in mind was the will of his Father which he had just accomplished by instructing the Samaritan woman about his

Father and himself. "That is my food," he told them.

Incidents like this in the life of Christ won for him the accusation—which was really a compliment—that he was the friend of sinners. We must let these incidents shape our own thinking about the people whom we know to be involved in disorders similar to the messed-up situation of the Samaritan woman. First of all, we have to avoid the hypocrisy of thinking proudly of ourselves as though we were not like the rest of men and as if our perseverance in faith in Christ were our own doing more than his. But then, granting that we are having some success in seeing ourselves as we really are, the problem remains about what to think and how to act when some member of the family or some good friend enters into a sinful relationship that is not really marriage. Sometimes when this happens, the father or mother disowns the son or daughter and refuses to have any association with them whatever. Maybe this is the best thing to do in certain cases, it's hard to say. But one is left wondering at times just what the main motive for such excommunications may be. Is it genuine concern for the erring and sinning member of the family or resentment over the injury to the family's reputation?

In forming our attitudes and planning our way of acting in this delicate matter, it is true that we must carefully avoid giving the impression that sin is not sin. But it is also good to reflect from time to time on the fact that Christ spoke with loving respect to the Samaritan woman. Her sins, real as they were, did not hide from him the value of the person who had sinned. By his willingness to talk with her in a matter of fact way, he kept the door open for her return to God.

Chapter 42

Devoted to Christ

ZEBEDEE and SALOME   (Mark 16)

THE gospels, which were written by men, make no secret
of the fact that in Christ's hours of greatest need it was
women rather than men who stuck by him. It was the women
of Jerusalem who unashamedly wept for him, while Simon,
the man from Cyrene, was forced to carry his cross. When
all the apostles had run for their lives in the garden where
Christ was arrested, only one of them, John, had the courage
to be seen at the foot of the cross. But with John there at the
cross were many women who were not afraid to offer their
dying Christ whatever comfort he would take from their
presence and love. Among these women was John's mother
Salome.

Her first knowledge of Christ came when she learned
that her two sons, James and John, had left their father
Zebedee and had gone off after Christ to learn his teaching
from his own lips and to take on whatever work he would
give them to do. This happened on the shore of the lake
of Galilee, where Christ had just called two other fisherman,
Peter and Andrew, to become his followers.

"Going on a little farther, he saw James son of Zebedee
with his brother John there in the boat preparing the fish
nets. Right away he called them. And they left their father

Zebedee in the boat with the hired help, and went after him." Salome must have wondered what it was in this man from Nazareth that had so powerfully attracted her two sons.

Soon Salome herself experienced this attraction and joined the growing school of men and women who were listening to Christ and learning his teaching. She did not stop being Zebedee's wife and the mother of her children. But she did spend all the time she could listening to Christ and serving his needs there in Galilee.

When Christ went with his apostles on that last trip to Jerusalem which was to bring him to his death, Salome went along together with some other Galilean women. During this time she became very dear to Christ. The gospels do not say this in so many words, but it is clear from something that happened.

One of Salome's sons, John, became the best loved of all Christ's apostles. John himself knew this, and in his own gospel he is referred to as the disciple whom Jesus loved. His brother James was also one of Christ's favorites. On special occasions, like the transfiguration and the raising of Jairus' daughter to life and the agony in the garden, James was one of the apostles picked by Christ to witness his glory or his power or his weakness. One day these two brothers, aware of their special standing with Christ, decided to ask him for special places in the Church which he was founding.

But even though they knew that Christ's special love for them gave them grounds for expecting him to listen favorably to their requests, they did not go to him directly but got their mother Salome to ask him for them. The fact that they asked her to go to Christ for them shows that she was as dear to him as they were and maybe dearer.

When she approached Christ and bowed low to honor him, he asked her what she had on her mind. She told him she hoped he would appoint her two sons to places of honor in his kingdom. When he asked the two of them if they could drink the cup of suffering with him, they told him they could. He assured them they would drink it. "You will drink my cup. But as for sitting at my right or left, I cannot give you this favor. It belongs to those for whom my Father has prepared it."

Mother and sons got his point: being a Christian is not so much a matter of receiving honors from Christ as of complete dedication—involving effort and sometimes pain—to his person. She was completely dedicated to him, and the fact that he set aside her request and gave her and her sons a lesson in humility should not obscure the fact of her closeness to him. Not long afterwards, she was to be standing watch at his cross.

On the first Easter morning Salome was one of the women who brought spices to the tomb of Christ in the hope of giving his corpse an unhurried and loving burial. To their shocked surprise they found the tomb empty. When the bewildering confusion of that day began to clear a little, she was among the first to feel the strange and unspeakable joy of Christ's resurrection; the women were convinced before the men. Salome had followed Christ faithfully all the way to the grave, and now the empty grave taught her that he was alive in a wonderful new way and that she was to continue following him, learning from him, loving him.

If the gospels were written for our instruction, this record of Salome's relationship with Christ must have a meaning for women today. Reading about her, they will gain a deeper understanding of their own relationship with Christ. Like her they will be attracted by Christ as he presents himself to them in his Church and in the gospels. Like Salome they will find the meaning of their lives in believing in

Christ, learning from him, loving him and serving his needs. Whether they are married or single they can give themselves as she did to him; as he in the first place has given himself to them. He gives himself to them most completely in the Mass and holy Communion by uniting them to himself as the body to its food; and he gives himself to them in their reading of the gospels by uniting their minds and hearts to his.

By loving her husband and serving his needs the Christian wife should know that she is also loving Christ and filling his needs. Saint Paul teaches this in his letter to the Ephesians. Christ presents himself to the Christian wife in the person of her husband; by loving her husband she loves Christ. By fulfilling her duties as a mother she is not only loving and caring for her children; she is also by that very love and care loving and caring for Christ who gives himself to her in her children. Surely what he said about seeing him in the least of his brothers means that a mother should see him and love him and serve him in her own children.

How rich the Christian woman's life will be, how full of the joy of Salome on the first Easter morning, if she keeps herself aware of the person of Christ in her home. And not only in her home but in all the people of her world she will find Christ needing her love and her service. And like Salome she will over and over again do all that she can to satisfy his needs. This is her vocation as it was Salome's. If she tries to live up to this vocation, she will be as dear to Christ as the wife of Zebedee was.

Chapter 43

Courage To Be Fair

PILATE and WIFE   (Matthew 27)

Every day the name of Pontius Pilate is on the lips of millions of Christians. They mention him every time they recite the Apostles' creed. If this Roman governor of Palestine about 30 A.D. could have known that he was to be remembered by this relentless dishonorable mention, his sad confusion on the day Christ died would have been even more embarrassing than it was.

Whether or not an oriental Christian tradition is right in holding that Pilate later became a great saint, we can't know for sure. We may hope that he did, and that the final word about this man will not be the one we say so often—"suffered under Pontius Pilate." Christ prayed for him and died for him; so there is good reason for our hope.

Pilate was a Roman loaded with the job of keeping order in a very troubled section of the Roman province of Syria. Jerusalem was the center of this trouble spot, and Pilate was particularly sensitive to any signs of rebellion there. For a good many years after 63 B.C. when the Roman armies conquered Palestine, the new masters of the Jewish people were generally easy in the demands which they made and they allowed the Jews a great deal of self-government. Slowly this condition changed. The Jews got tired of the Roman power over them, complained about it, plotted against it; and from time to time small groups of Jews broke out in armed rebellion. The Roman authorities reacted with more stringent controls.

Among these control measures was one which concerned the carrying out of penalties for crimes. For instance, although the Jewish religious court was allowed to condemn a criminal to death, it could not execute the death sentence; only the Roman authority, which at the time of Christ's death was Pontius Pilate, could take the condemned criminal's life.

Some knowledge of this conflict between Jew and Roman, which ended with a crushing defeat of the Jews in 70 A.D., is needed if we are to understand the problem Pilate had to face and the forces which proved too strong for his conscience.

The gospels make it clear that Pilate was the last in the line of those people who were responsible for killing Jesus. After a quick investigation of the case, Pilate was convinced that Jesus was not guilty of the charge made against him by the Jewish religious leaders, namely the charge that he was leading a rebellion against Roman authority in Palestine. He knew the real reason why they wanted Jesus destroyed; they were jealous of his popularity. And so Pilate indicated that he was eventually going to set the prisoner free.

But then they threatened to make trouble for Pilate in Rome, and fear changed his mind. He was afraid to act on his conviction about the innocence of Jesus. He passed the death sentence on a man whom he had just declared to be not guilty. If Pilate later became a saint, this was what he had to repent of and undo as best he could.

A problem arises whenever we ask about the causes of the death of Jesus. According to his own claim these human causes of his death are not the full explanation. Mysteriously hidden in the betrayal of Judas, in the malice of the Jewish religious leaders, in the careless lack of concern for justice on the part of the Jerusalem crowds, and in Pilate's cowardly fear—was Christ's own free will to die. However hard we may find this to grasp, there it is in his own words.

"The reason why my Father loves me is that I lay down my life so that I may take it up again. Nobody takes it away from me. Rather I lay it down of my own accord. I have the power to lay it down, and the power to take it up again. This command I have received from my Father."

But the fact that Jesus died by reason of a free decision on his own part should not obscure for us the fact that other free decisions—including Pilate's—must carry the responsibility for his death. It was Pilate who had the final say. And there is vast irony in the fact that among all those responsible ones the man who had least to gain had most to say.

No one would like to have been in Pilate's place—one man against the world. But not quite. Pilate did not have to feel that he was completely alone in wishing that Jesus would not be harmed. His wife was on his side. Her support was on his side. Her support was wobbly, and Pilate did not take any strength from it. Still it was there; she had offered it, hoping that in spite of all the threats, her husband would act as his conscience—and hers—urged him. Saint Matthew's gospel tells us that, while Pilate was still on the judgment seat his wife sent him this urgent message, "Don't involve yourself with this just man. I suffered a great deal in a dream today on account of him."

Pilate's wife must have known something about the danger which would involve her along with her husband if the Jewish leaders did not get what they wanted. Even so, she had the courage to ask her husband not to give them what they wanted, knowing that he might do what she asked.

What sort of dream it was that pained her in her sleep, what she knew about Jesus—these questions are not answered. But one thing is clear. She shared her husband's conviction that Jesus was a good man, and she made an effort to save his life. Both she and her husband had a sense of justice; but he lacked the courage to act justly.

Reading the gospel records on the part played by Pilate and his wife in the last days of Christ's life will remind husbands and wives today of their need for a sense of justice and for the courage to act accordingly. It is true that few men and women are faced with anything so dramatic or historically so important as the problem that landed on Pilate and his wife. But it is also true that a sense of justice and the courage to practice justice within the home are vitally necessary for the family's happiness. Justice is the habitual intention of giving to every other person what that person has a right to. When husband and wife give to one another what each has a right to from the other; when they give their children what they have a right to receive from them— in such a family there is a sense and practice of justice.

Sometimes in a family, mutual love, especially when it is felt with deep emotion, can make the virtue of justice seem cold and even unnecessary. But in the long run justice will keep things going right even when sharp conflicts arise or when the feeling of love disappears for a time.

Saint Paul was thinking along these lines when he told his Corinthian Christians that the very act of love which makes a man and his wife one flesh should be considered by them as a matter of justice. Such love is not only a favor given with all one's tenderness and with all one's strength, but also a debt to be paid and a duty to be done.

If at home we learn to practice justice as well as love, there is good reason to hope that we will practice justice in the larger human family of which we are a part.

Chapter 44

Lay Teachers of Religion

AQUILA and PRISCILLA   (Acts of Apostles 18)

THE Jews were expelled from Rome by the Emperor Claudius about 50 A.D. All through the fifties and sixties of the 1st century A.D. and up to the crushing of the Jewish revolt in Palestine in the year 70, the Jews of the Roman empire often found themselves driven from their homes.

Among the refugees who were pressured out of Rome by Claudius was a Jew named Aquila, who had moved to Rome from Pontus, in what is now Turkey. He and his wife Priscilla settled down at the big busy Greek city of Corinth, where they set up their business as tent-makers. Not long after they had made this new start, the apostle Paul arrived in Corinth during his second missionary journey.

Paul, too, was a tent-maker by trade and he supported himself by working at it. He met Aquila and Priscilla and entered into a business partnership with them. He lived at their home and worked with Aquila through the week. On the Sabbath, Paul would go to the local synagogue to see if he could get a hearing among the Corinthian Jews for his new teaching about Christ.

When, after many months, Paul decided to sail east for Palestine, his two friends accompanied him as far as Ephesus on the western coast of modern Turkey, where they settled down again. While they lived at Ephesus, they met a man who was to become one of the most brilliant Christian teachers in the first century, an Egyptian Jew named Apollo. He was a Christian when they met him, but his Christian formation had been incomplete; he had not yet heard of the Sacrament of Baptism! Saint Luke, in the 18th chapter of his Acts of the Apostles, where all this is recorded, writes, "On hearing him, Priscilla and Aquila took him in hand and explained the way of God to him more accurately."

From Paul's first letter to the Corinthians which was written from Ephesus, we learn that the home of Aquila and Priscilla became the regular place of assembly, or church, for the Christians of the city. Sometime later they were back in Rome, and again their house was being used as a church. The little church of Saint Prisca (Priscilla) on the Aventine hill in Rome today is a sign of their hospitality.

In Paul's letter to the Romans he greets these two friends and thanks them for having risked their lives for him on some occasion. Later they lived at Ephesus again. And when Paul, as an old man, wrote from his jail in Rome to Timothy, whom he had made Bishop of Ephesus, he greeted his old friends again.

These New Testament references to Aquila and Priscilla are skimpy enough. Still they tell us something important about this couple to whom Saint Paul was attached, with whom he lived and worked and traveled, of whom he thought when he wrote his letters to Corinth and Rome and to Timothy at Ephesus.

One incident stands out from all the rest—the instruction given by this couple to Apollo. Apollo's knowledge of Christ was deficient. So, they took it upon themselves to invite him to their home and teach him all they knew about Christ. They had learned from Paul, and maybe from other apostles too, and they in turn taught Apollo. Aquila was not a priest. He was a layman trying to make a living by working at his tent-making trade. And Priscilla was this tent-maker's wife. But they were lay people who took it for granted that they were called by God to take an active part in the life of the Church.

Saint Paul could not be everywhere; so they took his place and did his work for him whenever this was necessary. If they had not taken advantage of the opportunity of instructing Apollo, he might never have come all the way to Christ. If they had excused themselves on the grounds that they were lay people and therefore not equipped to teach anybody about religion, especially an intellectual like Apollo, he might never have become the capable instrument of bringing many others to Christ.

Saint Luke tells us that Apollo was of great service to the Christians of the first century. For this they had two alert and hard working lay apostles to thank. For who is to say how much their love for Saint Paul encouraged the great apostle in his work? Paul himself gives us a glimpse of the bond that united him to them when he writes that they risked their lives for him. In the Roman martyrology, which is the Catholic Church's official book on Saints, Aquila and Priscilla are honored on July 8. Tentmakers, teachers, saints —and they were married lay people.

Chapter 45

Parents Are Teachers

EUNICE and HUSBAND   (2 Timothy)

A NYBODY who reads the New Testament's Acts of the
Apostles will wonder where Saint Paul got all his
driving energy. One of the reasons why he could accomplish so much was the ability to put other people to work.
The assistant on whom Paul relied most was a much younger
man, named Timothy, whom Paul met at Lystra (in modern
Turkey) during his second missionary journey.

A few scattered references in the Acts of the Apostles and
in Paul's second letter to Timothy tell us something about this
man's family. His mother was a devout Jewess named
Eunice, his father was a gentile Greek. There was some
religious conflict in the family, since Timothy had not been
circumcised as a baby. But in spite of this defect, which was
about as serious for a Jewish family of that time as the
omission of baptism in a Catholic family today, she did a
good job of raising her son.

Saint Paul praises her great faith, and he mentions the
fact that Timothy had been carefully instructed in the Bible
from his earliest years. And there we have the main thing
known about Eunice. She was the first teacher of her son,
and she taught him the truths of the Jewish religion by in-
troducing him to the books of the Old Testament. Her

careful work as teacher of religion within her own home won for her Saint Paul's admiration and praise.

Whether Eunice and her gentile husband ever became Christians we do not know. But Saint Timothy could thank his mother for a thorough Old Testament preparation for the new teaching of Christ. Timothy's school was home, and his mother was its teacher.

All this reminds us of an urgent problem of the Catholic Church in the United States today—the religious education of Catholic children. Catholic parochial schools have for a long time played a vital part in this work, and the priests, sisters, brothers, and lay people who have built and run these schools are doing a work which is as important to the Church today as some of Saint Paul's work in his day. But the very success of these schools can be the occasion for some erroneous thinking. It sometimes happens that Catholic parents try to shift most of the responsibility for the religious education of their children onto the Sisters who teach in the parish school. The truth is that, even if all Catholic children of grade school age could attend Catholic schools, the first responsibility for teaching them about God and their relation to God would still rest on their parents. And many teaching Sisters will say that their work is seriously handicapped if the parents do not, by word and example, teach religion in their homes.

Timothy's mother did not shift the responsibility of educating her son onto the rabbis of the synagogue school at Lystra. From his earliest years she herself taught him about God and his relation to God by helping him to read and understand the books of the Bible. Are Catholic parents really less capable of doing as much for their children today?

One of the greatest Catholic biblical scholars of the 20th century enjoyed telling that when he was a very small child, too young to go to school, his mother would spend hours on winter evenings reading and explaining to her children the books of the Bible. The result was that by the time he started to school he was thoroughly acquainted with these books and had an understanding of their main doctrine. It is no wonder that he called his mother the most important teacher he ever had.

Some parents have underestimated their ability in the field of religion. They feel that they don't know enough about the Bible to use it in teaching their children. No doubt there is often a real basis for this attitude and a real need for a learning process on the part of the parents themselves. Materials are now available to help in answering this need. For instance, the Paulist Fathers of New York have published a series of pamphlet Bible commentaries aimed at helping the average reader to understand the books of the Old Testament. A similar series beginning with the New Testament has been published by Saint John's Abbey in Minnesota. Both these publications are efforts to bring the best of modern biblical scholarship to the service of ordinary readers of the Bible.*

If young Timothy was so useful as a helper of Saint Paul in his work of teaching the truths about Christ, this was due in no small way to his mother Eunice. What she did for her son can be done by mothers—and fathers—today.

* New Testament Reading Guide, The Liturgical Press, Saint John's Abbey, Collegeville, Minnestota; Pamphlet Bible Series, Paulist Press, 401 West 59th Street, New York 19, New York.

EPILOGUE

IF you have enjoyed thinking about the couples of the Bible and learning the lesson that God holds out to you through them, you must wonder when we are going to fix our attention on the most important couple of all. Joseph and Mary are real flesh and blood and bones like the others. And since they carried out a more important work than any of the others, they deserve to be called *the couple* of the Bible.

But their unique vocation as parents of Jesus, and in particular Mary's position as virginal mother, makes them so special that it seems best not to include them here as one couple among many others. The reader will open the gospels, especially the first two chapters of Saint Matthew and the first two chapters of Saint Luke, to find God's message about them.

The Christmas gospel has stamped their picture indelibly on our minds. "Joseph too went up from Galilee out of the city of Nazareth into Judea to the city of David which is called Bethlehem, since he belonged to the house and family of David. He went up to be registered with his espoused wife Mary, who was with child." We know only a little about them. But the little that we know is a treasure to be explored long and lovingly.